GUIDE TO COPYRIGHT AND INTELLECTUAL PROPERTY LAW

The Easyway

Calvin Lowe

Easyway Guides

Easyway Guides
Brighton BN2 4EG

© Straightforward Publishing 2008

ISBN 1847160 70 0
9781847160 70 6

Printed by Biddles Ltd Kings Lynn Norfolk
Cover design by Bookworks Islington

CONTENTS

Loco0199900i

INTRODUCTION

This Third Edition of A Guide to Copyright and Intellectual Property Law, The Easyway, deals comprehensively and clearly with a complex, elusive and rapidly changing area, of importance to those engaged in the commercial world, or to teachers of the subject.

The law of intellectual property impinges upon the lives of many people, whether traders, artists, musicians or designers. Whatever we do, whatever we create, we need to understand what protection the law affords our endeavours.

This brief book introduces the reader to the meaning of intellectual property and deals in depth with the various aspects of intellectual property such as:

-Patents and patent law, protecting the inventor
-Confidential information and breach of confidence,
-Trademarks, distinguishing one trader's goods from another
-Passing off, appropriating and damaging goodwill
-Character merchandising,
-Information Technology and intellectual property
-Copyright and infringement of copyright and, finally, design rights.

Overall, the reader, whether student or layperson, trader or artist, will benefit from the introduction offered in this book. The information is highlighted by examples of case law.

1

Intellectual Property Generally

Intellectual property is an area of law which is complex and rapidly changing.

In this first chapter we will examine the concepts and practice of intellectual property generally, in particular looking at:

- Differing areas of intellectual property
- Infringements
- Damages
- Criminal sanctions.

Throughout the rest of the book we will look at each area in detail.

Intellectual property rights is the overall term used to describe the various rights that afford protection to creative and innovative endeavour. There are a number of main rights, described in more detail throughout the book, including the following:

- Patents. This is a statutory property right that gives the patent holder the exclusive right to use certain inventions. A patent can be obtained by application to the patent office. Many people or organisations will use an agent to obtain a patent but it can be done on a do-it-yourself basis more cheaply. A patent will typically last up to twenty years.

- Trademarks. A registered trademark is, like a patent, a statutory right and gives the exclusive right to use a distinctive sign in relation to either a product or service. The sign can be a name, a symbol, aroma, jingle etc. A trademark can be obtained via an application to the Trade marks Division of the Patent Office. A trademark may be renewed indefinitely. Again, agents are used in the process but it can be carried out on a DIY basis.

- Copyright and moral rights. Copyright is a statutory right subsisting in original literary, dramatic, musical and artistic works and in sound recordings, films, broadcasts, cable programs and the typography of published editions. Owners of copyright will have economic rights within their works, including the important right to prevent unauthorised copying and adaptation. Moral rights are rights that authors retain in their works, irrespective of who owns the economic rights. Copyright varies according to its life span, usually the life of an author plus seventy years. Moral rights are personal to the author and arise automatically.

- Breach of confidence. The action for breach of confidence can be used to protect certain categories of confidential information, such as commercial information against unauthorised use or disclosure. The origins are contractual or equitable and the duration is indefinite or until the information is released into the public domain.

- Passing off. Goodwill is a form of property constituting the markets perception of the value and quality of a business and its products. This can be protected against interference or damage by what is known as 'passing off'. This is a tort that may be used in preventing a trader from making misrepresentations, which damages the goodwill of another trader. Again this is indefinite but ceases when the goodwill of a particular enterprise ceases.

- Design law. Certain aspects of the appearance of articles, aesthetic or non-aesthetic are protected via a combination of the registered design system, the design right (an unregistered design system) and aspects of copyright law. A registered design is the exclusive right to use certain features of a range of products. A design right is the right to prevent the copying of aspects of the shape or configuration of an article, such as a certain type of car. An unregistered design right will last up to fifteen years. A registered design, which can be granted upon application to the Designs Registry of the Patents Office, lasts up to twenty years.

Infringement of Copyright

The holder of an intellectual property right has to be in a position to enforce his or her rights if there is found to be an infringement of the IPR. In the main, civil remedies are available. However, certain infringements constitute a criminal offence. Remedies available after trial are known as final remedies. Interim remedies are also available, which are remedies awarded during trial. In relation to final remedies, financial remedies may take the form of damages or an account of profits.

Account of profits

This is a remedy involving the award to the right holder of the profits that the defendant has made from the infringement. This is a discretionary remedy and the right holder cannot gain both damages and account of profits. Where a right holder has the choice of electing to go for account of profits, that choice should be an informed one. In the case, Celanese International Corporation v BP Chemicals (1999), guidance on calculation of awards under accounts of profit was given, as follows:

a) The first step is to ascertain the total profits possible from the activities of the infringer.
b) The total profits should be apportioned to establish the ball-point profits (profit attributable to the infringement)
c) The resultant figure should then be adjusted to reflect the nature of the parties cases and:
d) Any tax paid should then be deducted.

Damages

This is the most common remedy for infringement. Usually they are based on lost profits or a royalty basis. The general rule is that they should be compensatory. They should put the party back in the position they would have been if the infringement had not occurred. Aggravated damages may also be available.

Non-pecuniary remedies

As follows:
a) Declaration. Declaratory relief (a declaration of infringement or of non-infringement) is discretionary.
b) Delivery up and destruction. In order to ensure that injunctions are properly effective, the court has the power to order delivery and destruction of infringing articles or require the defendant to destroy articles.
c) Discovery of names. This is a discretionary disclosure, known as a Norwich Pharmacal order (after Norwich Pharmacal

1974) which is made to an innocent third party requiring them to reveal the names of those that are ultimately responsible for the infringement.

d) Injunction. This is a court order at the court's discretion.

Interim remedies

Interim injunctions

An interim injunction is usually the most effective remedy for an IP right holder. To gain an interim injunction, the claimant should have an arguable case. Also, it should be seen that damages would not provide an adequate remedy. The courts should consider the balance of commercial convenience. If this is equal, the courts should act to preserve the status quo.

Ex parte orders

Inter parte proceedings (now known as proceedings on notice) are proceedings where the defendant has been served and has sufficient time to prepare his defences. In contrast, ex parte hearings (known as proceedings without notice) are hearings where only one side is represented. This party is under a duty of full and frank disclosure. Ex parte orders preserve the status quo pending a full hearing. There are two such orders that are relevant:

a) Search orders, formerly known as Anton Pillar orders after Anton Pillar (1976), the case where the first such order was granted). The grant of a search order allows the premises of an alleged infringer to be searched and evidence of infringement to be seized.

b) Freezing injunctions. These were formerly known as Mareva injunctions. These injunctions freeze the assets of an alleged infringer prior to trial (Mareva 1975) thus preventing transfer of assets.

Criminal sanctions

Intellectual property right remedies usually involve civil remedies but some criminal sanctions are available. The 2003 Copyright and related Rights Regulations, often known as the EU Copyright Directive amended the 1988 Copyright, patents and Designs Act to make it a criminal offence to infringe a copyright holders rights by making his or her work available to the public.

For the statutory IPR's, the individual statutes provide for criminal sanctions, e.g. the Copyright, Designs and Patents Act 1988 s.107 provides for imprisonment and fines for secondary infringement. Also, there is the general common law crime of conspiracy to defraud, which may be used in order to protect IPR.

2

Patents

....

In the previous chapter, we looked at intellectual property generally. We saw that it is a complex area. Throughout the rest of the book we will examine each area individually. In this chapter patents and patent law are explored, looking specifically at the following areas:

....

- The historical background to patents
- The definition of a patent
- Non-patentable inventions
- The concept of novelty
- State of the art inventions
- The inventive step
- The employee inventor
- Infringement of a patent
- Exceptions to infringement
- Applying for a patent

....

Historical background to patents and patent law

Patents were originally granted by the Crown exercising its Royal Prerogative. Letters patents were a royal proclamation that the bearer had the Crown's authority to do whatever had been authorised within the letters. The earliest record of a granted patent dates from 1331, to a Flemish weaver who wanted to practice his trade in England. Most of the patents granted at the time were to encourage trade rather than new inventions. In many cases, the grant of a patent was a way of controlling trade and towards the end of Elizabeth 1's reign, there were many abuses of the system.

The Statute of Monopolies 1623 was passed to control or limit these abuses. Monopolies per se were excluded unless they came within the exception in s.6. Under s.6 a 14-year monopoly could be granted for 'any manner of new manufacture'. The Patents Act 1835 was passed to deal with disclaimers and prolongations of claim, but the first comprehensive statute on the subject was The Patent Law Amendment Act 1852 which set up the Patent Office and Registrar of Patents. The Act also introduced the important requirement that a 'specification' be filed with an application describing the nature of the invention.

In 1883, the Patents, Designs and Trade Marks Act was passed to enable the United Kingdom to satisfy its obligations of reciprocity under the Paris Convention for the protection of Industrial Property. This Act required a full specification including detailed claims to be completed by the applicant and examined by the Patent Office before a patent would be granted. The case of Nobel's Explosive Company Limited v Anderson (1894) established that it was no longer possible to claim that the patent extended to matter contained within the specification where such matter was not in the claim. This highlighted the use of claims to mark the legal boundaries of the claim.

At this point in time, the United Kingdom patenting system was purely a deposit system, where applications were checked simply to make sure they had been completed correctly. The need to prove that an invention was really new did not come until the passing of the Patents Act 1907 which introduced the practice of checking patents for novelty, with searches being extended to cover patents granted over the last 50 years. The grounds for declaring a patent invalid were codified in the 1907 Act. In the 1919 Patents Act it was stated that invalid claims within an application would not invalidate the whole application.

The entire patents system was overhauled in 1949 by the Patents Act 1949, and the modern law on patents is set down in the Patents Act 1977, as amended by the 2004 and 2007 Acts, which was passed to satisfy the United Kingdoms Obligations under the European Patent Convention of 1973, the Community Patent Convention of 1975 and the Patent Co-operation Treaty of 1970. It contains sections outlining the procedures followed by the European Patents Office and plans for the Community patent.

It is to the Patents Act 1977 (as amended) that we will refer from hereon. The 2004 Act in particular has changed certain aspects of the 1977 Act such as employee's inventions.

The meaning of 'patent'
As we saw earlier, a patent is a monopoly right. The product or process, which is being patented, must first satisfy the criteria of the Act , which are:

1) There must be an invention, which must be capable of being patented but not an 'as such' invention. Certain inventions are non-patentable. This arises out of the Patents Act 1977 s1 (2) and (3)) The statute does not provide a clear definition of invention but the Patents Act

sets out a list of things that are considered to be inventions 'as such': general abstract entities, aesthetic and non-technical things are considered to be excluded. Discoveries, scientific theories and other things such as mathematical methods are not considered to be inventions 'as such'.

One of the most problematic areas to arise out of this definition of things that are not regarded as being true inventions is that of computer programs. Despite not being considered inventions under the Act it is the case that patents for software related inventions are indeed granted. Software patents are granted when a substantial technical contribution is made, as this is not considered to be a computer program as such. One of several approaches is taken when deciding whether there has been a technical contribution:

i) The question should be asked whether technical means are used to produce a result or solve a problem

ii) Does the invention produce a technical result

2) Novelty must be present in the product or process which distinguishes it from other products and processes (PA 1977 s.2)

3) An inventive step must be present, i.e. the product or process must be seen as containing an clear element of invention (PA 1977 s. 3)

4) The invention must be capable of industrial application, i.e. must be of a purpose which can be applied to some form of industry (PA 1977 s.4)

Other areas of enterprise are not patentable 'as such'. Mental acts, schemes, rules playing a game or business methods.

Mental acts. In Raytheon (1993) an apparatus and process was claimed for the identification of ships. This involved the digital composition of the silhouette of the unknown ship with silhouettes of known ships, held in a computer memory. The claim was held to be excluded as it was merely an automation of a method normally carried out by individuals, i.e. a mental act as such. Carrying out the method with a computer did not create a technical effect.

Schemes, rules or methods for playing a game. Innovations in this area do not really amount to a technical contribution.

Business methods. The courts in the UK have always taken a strict approach to the patentability of business methods. Inventions must make a technical contribution but that contribution must not be in an excluded thing (such as a business method) and it is also seen that advances in business methods are not technical. More recent European patent office developments indicate that a more relaxed approach may be adopted. Whilst process claims to business methods are not inventions, 'as such' product claims may be patentable.

The presentation of information
The Patents Act 1977 s.1 (2)(d) provides that means of presenting information are not inventions 'as such'.

Non-Patentable Inventions

In some cases, rare though they may be, the commercial exploitation of an invention may be contrary to public policy or morality. Such an invention is unpatentable. The European Patent Office in Harvard/Onco-mouse (1991) when considering the patentability of a mouse or other non-human mammal genetically engineered so as to be predisposed to develop cancer, suggested that this should be addressed as a balancing exercise. Here the suffering of the mouse and the possible environmental risks were felt to be outweighed by the utility of the invention to humans, hence the Onco-mouse was not immortal.

As public policy and morality objections proved particularly problematic in the field of biotechnology, Directive 09/44/EC on the legal protection of Biological Invention provides further guidance on what is not patentable:

1) The formation and development of the human body and mere discoveries of elements of the human body (this includes gene sequences) are not patentable. However, where a technical process is used to isolate or produce elements (including genes) from the human body, this may be patentable.

2) Processes for modifying human germ line genetic identity (i.e. genetic changes that can be passed to the next generation.

3) Human cloning processes.

4) Genetic engineering of animals which is likely to cause the animal to suffer without a substantial medical benefit, either to man or to animals.

5) Plant or animal varieties or biological processes for the production of such varieties are not patentable, but

inventions concerning plants or animals may be patented where the invention is not confined to a particular variety.

The concept of novelty

As discussed earlier, an invention must be novel (Patents Act 1977 s.1(1)(a) In UK patent law the terms 'novelty' and 'anticipation' are used interchangeably.

An invention must be new in the sense that it must not previously have been made available to the public The Patents Act 1977 s.2 (1) provides that an invention is novel where it does not form part of the state of the art. Anticipation is judged by asking 'is the invention part of the state of the art'? Novelty is assessed objectively. In order for an invention to be anticipated, the prior art must either contain an enabling disclosure (in the case of a product patent) or, for process patents, it must give clear and unmistakable directions to do what the applicant has invented.

State of the art

The Patents Act 1977 s.2 (2) defines the state of the art as comprising all matter made available to the public before the priority date of the invention, this being the date of the first patent application. It therefore comprises all knowledge, global, on the subject matter of the invention. This knowledge can be made available in any way, either written, orally, or by any other means before the priority date.

The state of the art includes matter included in earlier patent applications, including those patent applications that are not yet published. Everything in the state of the art is known as prior art. Novelty destroying prior art could include information that is part of common general knowledge as well as specific pieces of prior art.

In some circumstances, a known invention may still be patented where a new use for that invention can be found, for example first medical use (Patents Act 1977) which provides that the first medical use of a known compound is novel, providing that the medical application of the compound does not itself form part of the state of the art (s.2 (6). Also second medical use. In Europe a policy has developed of allowing second and subsequent uses of known compounds. Such claims are novel where the second or subsequent medical use does nor form part of the state of the art and provided the patent application takes a very narrow form known as a Swiss form claim i.e. the use of medicament X for treatment of disease Y. The UK courts have sanctioned the use of Swiss Form Claims, but second and subsequent medical uses will only be novel in the UK, where there is a new therapeutic application, discovering information about a medical use is sufficient.

The inventive step

An invention that is patentable must involve an Inventive step. An inventive step is present where an invention would not be obvious to a person skilled in the art. In patent law, the term's 'inventive step' and 'non-obviousness' are used interchangeably.

Inventive steps are assessed from the perspective of the person skilled in the art (PA 1977 s.3), the skilled man. This hypothetical person has certain attributes, he is the average person in the relevant art, possessing the relevant skills, knowledge and qualifications. The statutory test for inventive step is embodied in what is known as the 'windsurfer' test. This test follows the approach set out in Windsurfer v Tabur Marine (1983) as modified by PLG Research Ltd v Ardon International Ltd (1995). According to the Windsurfer test, to test obviousness the following should be asked:

1) What is the inventive step involved in the patent?
2) At the priority date, what was the state of the art relevant to that test?
3) How does the step differ from the state of the art?
4) Without hindsight, would the taking of the step be obvious to the person skilled in the art?

When attempting to obtain a patent, it is important to note that patents are territorial rights, not universal and therefore it is necessary to apply for patents in each jurisdiction for which protection is desired. For example, a UK patent may be obtained from the UK Patent Office. Although there is currently no 'European Patent' as such, a so called 'bundle' of patents, national patents, from states that are party to the European Patents Convention 1973 (EPC) may be obtained by a single patent application to the European Patent Office.

The employee inventor – ownership of patents

When a patent is applied for, the basic rules are that a patent must be granted to the following:

1) The inventor or joint inventors i.e. the actual devisor of the invention. (Patent Act 1977 s.7(2) (a)
2) The inventor(s) successors in title
3) The employer of an employee inventor.

Ownership of employee inventions

Inventors have the right to be mentioned as such but the Patent Act 1977 provides that where the inventors are employees their employer will own the invention if:

a) The invention was made in the course of the employee's normal duties or in the course of specially assigned duties, provided that he or she might reasonably be expected to carry out those duties.

b) Where the employee has a special obligation to further the interests of his employer's undertaking. This is related to the duty of fidelity that the employer owes to his or her employer.

Where the invention belongs to the employer, statutory compensation of the employer inventor may be available (PA 1977 s.40) provided that the patent is of outstanding benefit to the employer, the invention is subject of a patent grant and that is it just that compensation should be awarded.

There is a very high ceiling for statutory compensation and there has never actually been a reported case where statutory compensation under the 1977 act has been awarded. This is because such disputes tend to be settled out of court.

Patent applications may fail or those that are granted may be withdrawn on the basis of what is known as 'sufficiency'. A patent application consists of a number of components, and the patent specification is a vital part in which the invention is described and defined, it is the source of all the information about the patent that reaches the public domain. The specification must disclose the invention in such a way that the invention could be performed by the person skilled in the art. In other words, the application must contain an enabling disclosure.

The patent claim itself determines the scope of the monopoly granted to a patent proprietor. Claims must be clear and concise, be supported by the description and relate to a single inventive concept (PA 1977 s.14 (5)).

Infringement of a patent

Certain activities carried out in the United Kingdom without permission of the patent holder constitute infringement:

1) Primary infringement. This falls into three categories:

    i) where a product patent is at issue, making, disposing of, using, importing or keeping the patented product (or disposal or otherwise)

    ii) where a process patent is at issue, use of the process with actual or constructive knowledge that non-consensual use constitutes infringement

    iii) The use, offer to dispose of, importation or keeping for disposal or otherwise of a product directly obtained from a patented process.

2) Contributory infringement. The supply or offer to supply any of the means that relate to an essential element of the invention, for putting the invention into effect may constitute infringement. This will only be the case where there is actual or constructive knowledge that those means are suitable (and are intended) for putting the invention into effect in the UK.

Exceptions to infringement

There are a number of exceptions to patent infringement set out in the Patent Act 1977 s.60 (5)(a)-(i) the main ones being:

5) Private and non-commercial use
6) Experimental use

The courts have considered whether repairs to patented products constitutes infringement. The position is quite clear, genuine repair of a patented product that has been sold for use does not constitute infringement.

Anyone who wishes to attack a patent by claiming for revocation can do so on the grounds that the patent is not a patentable invention 'as such' or the invention is contrary to public policy or morality, the person granted the patent is not the person entitled to the patent, the patent specification does not amount to an enabling disclosure or there has been an impermissible amendment to the patent (PA 1977 s.72). Remedies for patent infringement are discussed in the previous chapter.

Now read the key points from Chapter 2 overleaf.

Key points from Chapter Two

- The modern law on patents is set down in the Patents Act 1977 (as amended)

- A protected patent is a monopoly right and must satisfy the criteria of the 1977 Patents Act.

- To be protected a patent must be original and novel.

- When inventors are employees the owner of the patent will be the employer. The employee may be entitled to some compensation.

- Certain activities carried out in the UK without the permission of the patent holder constitute infringement for which there are remedies.

3

Confidential Information, Breach of Confidence

....

In the previous chapter we looked at patent law. In this chapter we will look more specifically at confidential information and breach of confidence. In particular we will look at:

....

- The necessary quality of confidence
- Disclosure and the 'springboard doctrine'
- The obligation of confidence
- Non-contractual relationships
- Unauthorised use of information
- Defences
- Remedies

....

Confidential information

This area of law, covering confidentiality and breach of confidence, has developed through the common law and equity. From the mid-nineteenth century, the law has recognised that a breach of confidence can exist and has developed since that time.

The law is aimed at protecting secrets and should not be confused with laws available in other countries providing a right to privacy. It complements other aspects of intellectual property, as an obligation of confidence can arise even before the work in question is tangible. So, for example whereas the idea for a television program cannot attract copyright protection until it is recorded in some way, the person to whom the idea is disclosed can be prevented from publicising the idea to others or by exploiting the idea by the use of an action for breach of confidence. In Fraser v Thames Television (1984) three actresses and a composer devised an idea for a television series based on the story of three female rock singers who formed a band. They discussed the idea with Thames Television and offered Thames first option on the idea, subject to the three actresses being given the parts of three rock singers.

A dispute arose, and Thames made the program without engaging the actresses. The claimants claimed breach of confidence, with the defendants arguing that the idea disclosed was not entitled to protection unless it was a developed idea that had been recorded in some permanent form. The court did not agree-those requirements were more relevant to the issue of copyright protection-and accepted the claimants argument of breach of confidence. The judge did state that to be capable of protection by the law of confidence an idea must be 'sufficiently developed, so that it would be seen to be a concept which is capable of being realised as an actuality'.

The law of breach of confidence also protects an applicant for a patent by allowing him/her to impose an obligation of confidence on those who are in a position to know, or need to know, the details of the invention before a patent application is filed. This is important because if the details of an invention are made public before the patent application is made, as we have seen, it could fail for lack of novelty. Section 2 (4)(b) of the Patents Act 1977 states that publication made in breach of confidence will not invalidate the patent application.

The conditions for imposing an obligation of confidence were stated in Megarry j's decision in Coco v A.N. Clark (Eng) Ltd (1969). The claimant who had designed an engine for a moped entered into negotiations with the defendant company to discuss manufacture of the engine. All the details of the design were disclosed during these discussions. The parties subsequently fell out and the defendant decided to make its own engine, which closely resembled the claimant's. The claimant failed in his attempt to obtain an injunction to stop the defendant manufacturing the engine. Instead the court required the defendant to deposit royalties on sales of the engines into a joint account until the full hearing. According to the judge, to be able to claim breach of confidence, a claimant needed to satisfy three conditions. First, the information must have the necessary quality of confidence. Second, the information must have been imparted in circumstances importing an obligation of confidence. Third, there must be the authorised use of information. In the case described the court felt that only the second condition could be satisfied. Each condition now needs to be considered.

The necessary quality of confidence

The first condition is that the information must have the necessary quality of confidence. In other words, it should not be in the public domain. In a commercial or industrial context this might be a trade secret. A trade secret will cover technical information, like the mechanics of an invention that is yet to be the subject of a patent application If the information is so detailed that it cannot be carried in the head then it is a trade secret, but if it is simply a general method or scheme that is easily remembered then it is not.

Even where the information is not a trade secret, it can be classified as information of a confidential nature, if it has 'the necessary quality of confidence about it, namely it must not be something which is public property and public knowledge' (Lord Greene in Saltman Engineering Co v Campbell Engineering Co (1963).

The important point is that the owner of the information has not placed it in the public domain. Confidential information can come into the public domain in a number of ways, including by applying for a patent. When a patent is applied for, details of the patent application are published on the Patents Register.

Disclosure and the 'springboard doctrine'

General disclosure or publication of information will generally remove the obligation of confidence, a person who is under an obligation of confidence may be held under that obligation for a period. This is referred to as the springboard doctrine. One famous case here was Terrapin Ltd v Builders Supply Company (1967), the defendants made prefabricated portable buildings designed by the claimant. During the period of the agreement the claimant disclosed details of the design to the defendants in confidence. After the agreement ended the defendants produced their own buildings, which were similar to those produced by the claimant and the claimant claimed breach of confidence. Although the public could inspect the buildings at any time it was held that the defendant had acted in breach of confidence in that they should have not used information given in confidence.

Apart from the Springboard doctrine, it is important to consider exactly what is confidential and what is not. Essentially, notwithstanding the above, once information is released to the public then it is not confidential. For example, several rock stars and musicians, such as Tom Jones in Woodward v Hutchins (1977) were unable to stop the publication of details of their extra marital activities because they took place in public areas and were well known.

However, just because a secret is disclosed to another person that does not necessarily place it in the public domain. One case that illustrated this is Stephens v Avery (1988) where the claimant confided to a friend that she had been involved in a lesbian relationship with the deceased wife of a known criminal. The so-called friend disclosed the information to a Sunday newspaper, claiming that the disclosure to her meant that the information ceased to be confidential. The judge, Sir Nicholas Browne-Wilkinson held that:

'The mere fact that two people know a secret does not mean that it is not confidential. If, in fact, information is secret, then in my judgement it is capable of being kept secret by the imposition of a duty of confidence on any person to whom it is communicated. Information only ceases to be confidential when it is known to a substantial number of people'.

It is clear that if a person is told something as a secret then they are under an obligation to keep that information confidential until it is clearly in the public domain.

The obligation of confidence

A second condition that arose out of Coco v Clark is that the information must have been 'imparted in circumstances importing an obligation of confidence'. In this case it is important to look at the relationship between the person imparting the information and the person who receives it. The relationship can be based on contract, trust, friendship or also marriage.

In contractual agreements the parties may have confidentiality clauses in their contracts Even if there are no express terms the parties to the contract may be under an obligation of confidence which is implied. Pre-contractual disclosures can also be binding even if no contract materialises. One such case highlights this and that is Tournier v National Provincial and Union Bank of England (1924), it was held that the bank was under an obligation of confidence to its customers, unless required to disclose information by law.

Contracts of employment impose or imply quite clear duties of confidence. However, importantly, there is no duty to keep a secret about an employer's wrongful or unlawful acts. The obligation of confidence can continue even after the contract of employment has come to an end. One important case highlighting this was Faccenda Chicken Ltd v Fowler (1986) the claimant who sold fresh chickens from refrigerated vans, applied for an injunction to prevent two former employees from using their knowledge of sales, prices and customers details, when they set up a competing business. The judge said that in deciding whether the former employees owed a duty of confidence in respect of this information a number of factors should be considered:

- the nature of the employment. Was confidential information habitually, normally or only occasionally handled by the employer?

- The nature of the information itself: only trade secrets or information of a highly confidential nature would be protected.
- Whether the employer impressed upon the employee the confidential nature of the information.
- Whether the relevant information could be isolated easily from other information that the employee was free to use or disclose.

While one of the employees in question was employed there was information that could be regarded as confidential and could not be disclosed by him, or used for any other purpose as it was in breach of contract. However, when the contract of employment ended, such information that had become part of his own skill and knowledge ceased to be confidential and the employee was entitled to make use of that information and those skills. Independent contractors, while not under a contract of employment, are usually under a duty of confidence by virtue of terms expressed or implied by law in a contract for services.

Non-contractual relationships

The obligation of confidence is not restricted to contractual relationships. For example it can apply between doctor and patient, subject to public interest defence. A secret between friends can give rise to an obligation of trust. This was highlighted in Stephens v Avery, as described. What ties the different relationships together is that, as stated in Coco v Clark by J Megarry:

'The circumstances are such that any reasonable man standing in the shoes of the recipient of the information would have realised that upon reasonable grounds the information was given him in confidence'.

Another test was applied in Carflow Products (UK) Ltd v Linwood Securites (Birmingham) Ltd (1966) where the judge use a subjective test, i.e. what obligations did the parties intend to impose and accept? In that case, because both parties wanted to invalidate a third party's registered design right by showing that it had been previously been available in the public domain, both party's agreed that they did not intend the information to be treated as confidential. The judge also imposed an objective test that could be used if the subjective test was not answered. This test was the same as that used in the Coco v Clark case.

The obligation of trust will extend to third parties if it is obvious that the information is of a confidential nature. For example, as in cases such as Stephens and Avery. The media is under an obligation not to publish information of a confidential nature passed on by a recipient. In the same way, where an ex-employee is under an obligation of confidence the new employer will be too.

Unauthorised use of information

Megarry J's third condition in Coco v Clark was that the information has been used without the owner's authority. Within an agreement involving obligations of confidence, there will be implied as well as express terms. It will be clear that certain information is confidential. However, it may be necessary to disclose the information to others not directly party to the agreement. For example, where one party is engaged to manufacture the subject of the agreement, employees on the shop floor will need to have access to the information covered by the agreement in order to produce the end product, as well as sub-contractors. The authority to disclose in this instance will be implied into the agreement, even if not expressly contained.

One other question to be asked is, can a co-owner of information prevent its use by other co-owners?

In Drummond Murray v Yorkshire Fund managers Ltd and Michael Hartley (1998) this was clearly illustrated. The claimant was a marketing expert involved in the purchase of companies. He joined a team of five for the purpose of management buy out/in of a company. The group created a business plan to interest venture capitalists. The business plan and the price to be paid for assets were highly confidential. Each member of the group was a co-author of the business plan with equal rights in it. However, there was no agreement between group members as to how this confidential information should be used.

The group approached the defendants as potential investors. The business plan and the price to be paid for the assets were discussed. The first defendant was interested in investing in the company but questioned the claimant's involvement as managing director and the group, other than the claimant, agreed for the latter to be replaced by the second defendant. The claimant sued for breach of confidential information, contending that the confidential information was given to the defendants for the purpose of deciding whether to invest. The second defendant was therefore not entitled to use that information for any other purpose and had breached this obligation by using this information for the purpose of replacing him as managing director. The Court of Appeal held that the confidential information was incidental to the relationship between the group members. The confidential information ceased to be the claimant's property once this information was dissolved. As there had been no agreement between group members the claimant could not prolong that relationship once he ceased to be a group member.

Defences

Confidential information and the public interest

The only real defence to this form of action is that disclosure of the information is in the public interest. As with copyright, the law of confidence is not available to protect confidential information that is considered immoral.

Remedies

Damages for breach of confidence will generally be calculated on the basis of compensating the claimant for the conversion of property. There are many ways to arrive at a sum for compensation and this will depend on the individuals case and loss incurred. The Court of Appeal, in Indata Equipment Supplies Ltd v ACL Ltd (1998) stated that damages should be assessed on a tortious basis, that is such sum as would put the claimant into the position he would have been had it not been for the tort, or breach of confidence.

As with infringement of other intellectual property rights, the claimant can request an account of profits where the information has been used commercially. This is an equitable remedy that is at the courts discretion, as is an order for the delivery up and destruction of goods made using the confidential information.

As this area of law is concerned with confidential information, the usual remedy sought is that of an injunction preventing disclosure of information, if this is practical and the information is not already in the public domain.

Now read the key points from Chapter 3 overleaf.

Key points from Chapter Three

- The are of law relating to confidential information and breach of confidence has developed through the common law and equity since the mid-nineteenth century.

- General disclosure or publication of information will generally remove the obligation of confidence.

- The obligation of confidence is not restricted to contractual relationships, it can also be between individuals.

- The remedies for breach of confidence are usually damages. Injunctions can also be obtained.

4

Trademarks

....

In the previous chapter we examined the areas of confidentiality and breaches of confidence. In this chapter we look specifically at trademarks and the law. In particular we will look at the following areas:

....

- Definition of a trademark
- Historical background
- International provisions
- The Community Trademark System
- Registration of trademarks
- Collective marks
- Trademark law
- Classification of a trademark
- Marks that cannot be registered
- Infringements of a trademark

....

Definition of a trademark

A trademark is a symbol or a sign placed on, or used in relation to, one trader's goods or services to distinguish them from similar goods or services supplied by other traders. Section 1 of the Trade Marks Act 1994, which is the main legislation covering trade marks, defines a trade mark as any sign capable of being represented graphically which distinguishes the goods or services of one business from those of another.

The enactment of the 1994 Act radically changed the law dealing with registered trademarks. The legislation harmonises the trade mark law of the United Kingdom with that of the rest of the European Community and implements the first council directive (89/104/EEC) to approximate the laws of the member states relating to trademarks. The Government also took the opportunity with the 1994 Act to bring the law up to date, as the previous Act the 1938 Act was inadequate in its scope and coverage.

Historical background

Traders have, from the earliest times, distinguished their goods by marking them. By the 19th century it had become very clear that marks applied to goods that had become distinctive had an intrinsic value and needed some form of legal protection lacking at the time. Such protection was available through the use of Royal Charters and court action, which involved injunctions or action for infringement, although clearly this was not adequate or far reaching enough.

The Trademark Registration Act 1875 was passed to overcome the difficulties encountered in court actions. The Act established a statutory Register of Trademarks that is still in use today. The Register provides the trademark owner with proof of title to, and exclusive rights of use of, the trademark for the goods in respect of which it is registered. The Act of 1875 also laid down the essentials of a trademark.

A number of Acts followed, the Patents, Designs and Trademarks Act 1883, the Trademarks Act 1905 and the Trademarks Act 1919. These Acts culminated in the 1938 Trademarks Act which in turn was replaced by the 1994 Trademarks Act.

International Provisions

There are a number of international conventions and arrangements that give some international recognition to national trademarks. These are The Paris Convention, The Madrid Arrangement and the Protocol to the Madrid arrangement (Madrid Protocol). There is also a Community Trademarks System that creates a trademark that gives rights throughout the European Community and which will be referred to below.

Paris Convention

The Paris Convention came into being in 1883. Its overall purpose was to create recognition between various countries of each other's national intellectual property rights, through the concept of priority.

Priority recognises the first filing date for a particular intellectual property right in any convention country as the filing date for all other convention countries in respect of the same property right. The period of priority differs from intellectual property right to intellectual property right but for trademarks the period is six months. This has given a level of international protection for trade marks because the first to file a trade mark application is, in most countries, the person with better claim to a trade mark.

In England, this is not the case because rights in passing off (see later) can be built up through sufficient use of a trademark, without registration, and these rights can act as an obstacle to any subsequent application to register the trademark by a third party.

Another provision of the Paris Convention relevant to trade marks is Article 6, which gives international protection to 'well known' trademarks. A person can own a well-known trademark in registered or unregistered form even in countries where the action of passing off does not exist. Ownership of a well known mark will prevent a third party from applying to register the same or similar mark in any other convention country that has implemented Article 6 and allows cancellation of an existing registration for such an identical or similar mark during the first five years after registration on the application of the owner of the well known mark.

The Madrid Agreement

The Madrid Agreement was implemented in 1891 to simplify the procedure for filing trademark registration in many countries. The Madrid Agreement aimed to replace the multiple filing of trademark registrations in (10) individual countries.

The Madrid Agreement allows anyone established or domiciled in an Agreement country, with a trademark registration in his or her country, to file one international application that will cover all Madrid Agreement countries. The central application is filed with the offices of the World Intellectual Property Rights Organisation (WIPO) in Geneva. This is then administered by that office. England did not sign the Madrid Agreement so this is not available to English trademark owners.

The Madrid Protocol

As a number of key countries did not sign the Madrid Agreement, discussions began in the mid-1980's on how to make the Madrid system more palatable. The result was the Madrid Protocol established in 1989. At the current time there are 42 signatories to the protocol including the UK. Up to date information concerning the countries and the protocol see www. Itma.org.uk

The protocol is based on essentially the same structure as the Madrid Agreement, with a few differences designed to allow more flexibility.

Community Trademark System

Although classed as an international registration system, the CTM operates differently from either the Madrid Agreement or Madrid Protocol. It is more like the national system (see below) in that it is a means of filing an application for one trade mark at one trade mark registry to obtain one registration under one set of laws and procedures. The only difference is that the area covered by the registration is a collection of countries within the European Union.

The application can be filed in The CTM Office in Alicante Spain or at the National Trademark office in any member country, which passes the application to the CTO Office.

Trademarks and registration of trademarks

As discussed, the function of a trademark is to distinguish between one trader's goods and another trader's goods. The function of an ordinary trade mark is to act as an indicator of trade origin, which aids both consumers of branded goods and the trade mark proprietor, as follows:

1) The trademark acts as an indicator of quality and reliability, protecting consumers from confusion or deception in the market place.
2) The trademark can be enforced to protect the mark's proprietor against certain acts of unfair competition.

Collective marks and certification marks

Although they are rare, such trademarks perform different function compared to ordinary trademarks. Certification marks (Trademarks Act 1994 s.50) are intended to indicate that goods or services comply with a certain objective standard as to quality, origin, material, the mode of manufacture of goods or the performance of services or other characteristics. Any third party whose goods or services meet the required standards may apply to be an authorised user of a certification mark and the proprietor cannot refuse this request.

Collective marks serve to indicate members of an association. A third party who is not a member of that association does not have the right to use the mark. Collective marks can act as certification marks and vice versa.

Trademark law

As seen, in the UK, trademarks are governed by the 1994 Trademarks Act. An application for a national trademark may be made to the Trademark Registry (part of the UK Patent Office). Community Trademarks (CTM), a trade mark that is valid in the entire EU, may be obtained from the CTM Office, The Office for Harmonisation in the Internal Market (Trademarks and Designs) (OHIM). Not all marks are capable of being registered as trademarks. Objections to the registration of a mark may be raised, either by the Trademarks Registry during examination of the mark or by third parties during any opposition actions or proceedings. The grounds for refusing registration are divided into two categories:

a) Absolute grounds for refusal (TMA 1994 s.3 and 4) which are concerned with objections based on the mark itself.
b) Relative grounds for refusal (TMA 1994 s.5) these being concerned with a conflict and third party rights.

Classification of a trade mark

The Nice Agreement for the International Classification of Goods and Services provides that there are thirty-four classes of goods and eight classes of services. Any application for registration must stipulate which classes, or sub-classes, in which registration is sought. Multi-class applications are possible and it would, in theory, be possible to register a mark in respect of all forty two classes.

However, this is very unlikely as applicants must have a bona fide intent to use the marks for the prescribed goods and services (TMA 1994 ss.3 (6) and 32 (3)).

Limited registration for retail service marks is also now possible in class 35. This change follows OHIM's decision in Giacomelli Sports Spa (1999).

Definition of a trade mark

The 1994 Trademarks Act s.1(1) provides that a trade mark is a sign capable of being represented graphically, capable of distinguishing goods or services of one undertaking, from those of another undertaking. There are a number of elements in the definition:

a) *A 'sign'.* The concept of a sign in UK trademark law is very broad indeed. Although there is no clear definition, signs provided in the UK include works, designs and shapes and also more unconventional marks such as sounds and smells. A sign can be regarded as anything that conveys information (Phillips v Remington (1998) See below.

b) *Graphic representation.* Signs must be represented graphically, i.e. be represented in such a way that third parties may determine and understand what the sign is,. This requirement is normally satisfied by including an image of the mark in the trade mark application. However, it has been suggested that provision of an image is not absolutely necessary provided that third parties can clearly identify the mark from the description (Swizzels Matlow Ltds Application (1999). It may be difficult to graphically represent unconventional marks, but practice dictates for example that sound marks are represented by music notation and that for shape marks it is best to submit line drawings or photographs. Applications for colour marks will usually include a representation of the colour and so on.

c) *Capable of distinguishing.* Signs must be capable of distinguishing goods or services of one undertaking from another undertaking. Any sign that has the capacity to distinguish will satisfy this requirement.

Absolute grounds for refusal
A sign will not be registered if it falls within one or more of the absolute grounds for refusing registration.

Signs not satisfying the s.1 (1) requirements

Signs which do not meet the definition of 'trade mark' provided in the Trademarks act 1994 will not be registered. In addition, it is important for an applicant not to make a mistake as to the graphic representation as the opportunities to correct or amend are very limited (TMA 1994 s.39 prevents the correction of errors in a trade mark application that would substantially affect the identity of the trade mark). This is mitigated by the fact that it is Registry practice to examine marks for graphic representation before a filing date is allocated.

Scent marks continue to cause considerable difficulties for graphic representation. John Lewis Application (The scent of Cinnamon) (2001) indicates a description of a scent is unlikely to be precise enough.

Signs must also be capable of distinguishing the goods or services of one undertaking form those of other undertakings. As noted above, this is not a high standard and, in effect, it will only bar those signs that are incapable of functioning as trademarks (e.g. the Philips shaver shape in Philips Electronics v Remington Consumer products (1999) a case discussed below, was held not to be distinctive in a trade mark sense and thus did not satisfy TMA 1994, s.3 (1)(a)).

Marks devoid of distinctive character or those consisting of exclusively descriptive or generic signs are prohibited unless it can be shown that before the application was made, a mark has acquired a distinctive character as a result of a use made of it. This proviso to the TMA 1994 ss.3 (1)(b)(c) and (d) means that there is no absolute prohibition as a matter of law on non-distinctive, descriptive and generic marks. As recognised in

British Sugar v James Robertson (TREAT) 1996, such marks may be registered where they have become factually distinctive upon use despite the provisions stated in the TMA 1994 s.3 (1)(b)-(d).

This proviso does not apply to TMA 1994 s.3(1)(a) or any other absolute ground for refusal.

Marks devoid of distinctive character

TMA 1994 s.3 (1)(b) prevents the registration of marks that are not, prima facie, distinctive. An example might include a surname common in the UK. In British Sugar v James Robertson (TREAT) 1996, it was said that a mark is devoid of distinctive character where the sign cannot distinguish the applicants goods or services without the public being first educated that it is a trademark. The mark at issue in this case, TREAT, for a syrup for pouring on ice cream and desserts, was therefore devoid of distinctive character. Such marks may, nevertheless, benefit from the TMA 1994 s.3 (1)(b) proviso. Therefore trademarks will only fail where they are not distinctive by nature and have not become distinctive by nurture.

Signs that are exclusively descriptive

For a sign to be open to objection under TMA 1994 s.3 (1)(c) the trademark must consist exclusively of a sign which may be used in trade to describe characteristics of the goods or services. The sub-categories of TMA 1994 s.3 (1)(c) are:

1) Kind. Terms indicating kind or type that should be free for all traders to use, e.g. PERSONAL for computers, are not normally registrable.

2) Quality. Laudatory words, e.g. PERFECTION, are not usually registrable.

3) Quantity. The Trade marks Registry gives the example that 454 would not be registrable for butter, as butter is frequently sold for domestic consumption in 454g (1lb) packs. Where numerical marks are not descriptive or otherwise objectionable, they may be registered.

4) Intended purpose. Generally, words referring to the purpose of goods or services are not registrable.

5) Value. Signs pertaining to the value of goods or services are not normally registrable, e.g. BUY ONE GET TWO FREE.

6) Geographical origin. Geographical names are not usually registrable unless used in specific circumstances.

7) Time of production of goods or the rendering of services. Typically, marks such as SAME DAY DELIVERY for courier services or AUTUMN 2004 for haute couture would not be registrable.

8) Other characteristics of goods and services. For example, a representation of the good or service would not usually be registrable.

Marks falling into any of these categories may still be registrable if they have become distinctive upon use.

Signs that are exclusively generic

TMA 1994 s.3(1)(d) prohibits the registration of signs or indications that have become customary in the current language or in the bone fide and established practices of the trade. An example can be found in JERYL LYNN Trademark (1999) where an application for JERYL LYNN for vaccines was refused as the mark described a strain of vaccine and was not distinctive of the applicant.

Shapes that cannot be registered

Traditionally in the UK, shapes were not registerable. One case highlighting this was Coca-Cola's trademark application (1986).

However, the TMA 1994 makes it very clear that the shapes of goods and their packaging are now registrable (TMA 1994 s.1 (1)), but the TMA 1994 s.3 (2) excludes certain shapes from registration. This is an area of trademark law that has lacked clarity.

ECJ guidance on the registrability of shape marks has clarified matters somewhat. The UK Court of Appeal stayed proceedings in Phillips Electronics v Remington Consumer products (1999) to allow a preliminary reference to the ECJ in a number of issues, including questions specific to shape marks and this decision has implications for the interpretation of the TMA 1994 s.3 (2). In this case, Philips had been producing a three-headed rotary shaver for a considerable time (the Philishave). When Remington produced a rotary shaver of a similar design Philips sued for infringement of a mark which was the face of the three headed shaver.

The TMA 1994 provides that the following shapes are not registrable:

1) Where the shape results from the nature of the goods themselves. Inherent shapes therefore cannot be registered. In the Philips case, The Court of Appeal considered that there would be no objection to Philips three headed shaver shape on this ground as electronic shavers can take other forms.
2) Where the shape of the goods is necessary to achieve a technical result (TMA 1994 s.3 (2)(b). Functional shapes are

therefore not registrable. In Philips 1999 case it was considered that the shaver shape was necessary to achieve a technical result, but the ECJ was, nevertheless, asked to adjudicate in the matter, i.e. on the correct approach to functional shapes. The concurred in the matter. They also confirmed that the fact that there may be more than one shape that could achieve the same result is not relevant. Consequently, it appears that only shapes with specifically non-functional aspects are registrable.

3) Where the shapes gives substantial value to the goods. In Philips (1999) the Court of Appeal suggested that a valuable shape in this context can be identified where the shape itself adds substantial value, e.g. the shape adds value via eye appeal or functional effectiveness. In contrast, shapes that are valuable because they are 'good trademarks' would not fall foul of the TMA 1994.

Marks likely to give offence or deceive

A mark will not be registered if it is contrary to public policy or accepted principles of morality (TMA 1994 s.3 (3)(a) or is of such a nature that it is likely to deceive the public. For example, as to the nature, quality or origin of the goods or services.

Relatively few marks are deemed to be contrary to public policy or morality. Morality should be considered in the context of current thinking and only where a substantial number of persons would be offended should registration be refused.. For example, in BOCM's application, (EUROLAMB) (1997) EUROLAMB was considered to be deceptive if used in relation to non-sheep meat (when used in relation to sheep meat it was descriptive). It is very clear that the test of deception is deceptive and actual evidence of deception must be provided.

Marks prohibited by UK or EC law

The registration of marks whose use would be illegal under UK or Community law is precluded by TMA 1994 s.3(1)(d).

Protected emblems

TMA 1994 s.4 provides details of marks that are considered to fall into the category of specially protected emblems, e.g. marks with Royal connotations, and the Olympic symbol cannot be registered. Marks containing such emblems cannot be registered without consent.

Applications made in bad faith

There is no requirement that a mark need be used prior to the application for registration, but the applicant must have a bona fide intention to use the mark TMA 1994 s.32 (3) and applications may be refused when they are made in bad faith. Therefore, so-called ghost applications should be caught buy this section.

Relative grounds for refusal

The applicant must also overcome the relative grounds for refusing registration. These relate to conflict with earlier marks or earlier rights. The 'earlier mark' (TMA 1994 s.6) might be a trademark registered in the UK or under the Madrid Protocol. Alternatively it might be a CTM or a well-known mark (the latter are entitled to protection as per article 6 of the Paris Convention for the Protection of Industrial Property 1883).

There is no provision for honest concurrent use in the TMA 1994. As it has been made clear that a trade mark application must be refused, irrespective of honest concurrent use, if the registered proprietor objects, this provision is of limited value to the applicant. If the proprietor of the registered mark objects, honest concurrent use provides no defence.

Conflict with an earlier mark for identical goods or services

The TMA 1994 s.5 (1) only provides the narrowest relative ground for refusing registration: a mark identical to an earlier trademark and used for identical goods and services will not be registered. The requirement of 'identical goods and services' is sufficiently broad in scope to include cases where the applicants mark is identical to only some of the goods and services for which the earlier mark is registered, but to 'constitute an 'identical mark' a very high level of identity between the marks is required. One such case highlighting this is Origins Natural Resources v Origins Clothing (1995).

The registration of similar marks for the same or similar services is only prohibited where confusion on the part of the public is likely to arise (TMA 1994 s.5 (2). Specifically what is prohibited is the registration of:

1) Identical marks for similar goods or services or
2) Similar marks for identical/similar goods or services where, because of the identity or similarity, there is a likelihood of confusion on the part of the public, which includes the likelihood of association with the earlier trade mark.

What constitutes 'confusing similarity' has been considered at length by the ECJ (Sabel v Puma 1998) and Canon v Metro Goldwyn Meyer (1999). Confusion has to be appreciated globally taking into account all factors relevant to the case. These factors include:

- The recognition of the earlier trade mark on the market
- The association that can be made between the registered mark and the sign
- The degree of similarity between the mark and the sign and the goods and the services, the degree of similarity must be considered in deciding whether the similarity is sufficient so as to lead to a likelihood of confusion

It has also been made clear that 'likelihood of association' is not an alternative to 'likelihood of confusion" but serves to define its scope. This means that if the public merely makes an association between two trademarks, this would not in itself be sufficient for concluding that there would be a likelihood of confusion. There is no likelihood of confusion where the public would not believe that goods or services came from the same undertaking.

Conflict with a mark of repute

A mark that is identical or similar to an earlier mark will be refused registration in respect of dissimilar goods or services where the earlier mark is a mark of repute and the use of the later mark would, without the cause, take unfair advantage of or be detrimental to the reputed mark's distinctiveness or reputation. (TMA 1994 s5 (3).

A mark of repute is a mark with a reputation in the UK (for CTM applications it must have a reputation in the EU. In deciding as to whether a trade mark has a reputation, the ECJ has provided some guidance (General Motors Corp v Yplon (2000). Repute would be judged with reference to the general public or to a specific section of the public, and the mark must be known to a significant portion of that public. Relevant indicators of the public's knowledge of the mark include the extent and duration of the trade marks use, its market share and the extent to which it has been promoted.

In order for registration to be refused under s.5 (3) use of the applicants mark will have to take unfair advantage of or be detrimental to the reputed marks distinctiveness or reputation. In OASIS STORES LTD's application (EVEREADY) (1998) it was said that merely being reminded of an opponents mark did not itself amount to taking unfair advantage. The fact that the applicant did not benefit to any significant extent from their opponent's reputation and the wide divergence between the parties goods was relevant, s.5 (3) could not be intended to prevent the registration of any mark identical or similar to a mark of repute.

Conflict with earlier rights

TMA 1994 s.5 (4) provides that where a mark conflicts with earlier rights, including passing off, design rights and copyright the mark will not be registered.

Surrender, revocation, invalidity, acquiescence and rectification

It is possible to surrender a trademark with respect to some or all of the goods or services for which it is registered. Marks may be revoked (removed from the registry on three grounds: non-use because the mark has become generic; or because the mark has become deceptive. A mark will be invalid if it breaches any of the absolute grounds for registration. Where the proprietor of an earlier trade mark or other right is aware of the use of a mark subsequently registered in the UK and has, for a continuous period of five years, taken no action regarding that use the proprietor is said to have acquiesced. Where this is the case, the proprietor of the earlier mark or right cannot rely on his right in applying for a declaration of invalidity or in opposing the use of the later mark, unless it is being used in bad faith. Anyone with sufficient interest can apply to rectify an error or omission in the register. Such a rectification must not relate to matters that relate to the validity of the trademark.

Infringement

The proprietor (and any exclusive licensee) has certain rights to a mark (TMA 1994 s.9 (1) which are infringed by certain forms of unauthorised use of the mark in the UK. These rights come into existence from the date of registration, which is the date of filing. All infringement acts require the mark to be used in the UK in the course of trade. What constitutes 'use' of a mark has been the subject matter of some debate and is discussed below.

Use of an identical sign for identical goods or services

Use, in the course of trade, of an identical sign, in respect of goods or services constitutes trademark infringement (TMA 1994 s.10 (1).

Use of an identical or similar sign on identical or similar goods or services

Use, in the course of trade, of an identical sign or similar goods or services (TMA 1994 s.10 (2) (a) or a similar sign on identical goods or services constitutes infringement where the public is likely to be confused as to the origin of goods or services or is likely to assume that there is an association with the registered mark.

Use of a mark similar to a mark of repute for dissimilar goods or services

Registered marks with a 'reputation' are infringed if an identical or similar mark is used for non-similar goods or services, where the use takes unfair advantage of or is detrimental to, the distinctive character or repute of the distinctive mark (TMA 1994 s.10 (3).

Contributory infringement

TMA 1994 s.10 (5) is known as the contributory infringement provision. This provision creates a form of secondary participation where a person who applies a trademark to certain materials has actual or constructive knowledge that the use of the mark is not authorised. This provision extends infringement down the supply chain, but printers, publishers, manufacturers or packaging etc. may avoid a s. 10 (5) liability in practice by inserting suitable contractual forms into their agreement with their clients.

Defences to infringement

a) Comparative advertising. Comparative advertising is allowed under certain circumstances as long as the use is not unfair or detrimental. One such case that highlights this is British Airways PLC v Ryanair Ltd (2001). British Airways had brought an action for infringement against Ryanair for the publication of two Ryanair advertisements comparing fares with BA. The courts found that, in assessing as to whether a mark has been used in accordance with honest practice, the court should view the advertisement as a whole. Although misleading adverts cannot be honest, on the facts, whilst the advertisement at issue may have caused offence it was not dishonest and the price comparisons were not significantly unfair.

b) The use of another registered mark. The use of one registered mark, within the boundaries of the registration, does not infringe another registered mark.

c) Use of own name or address. A person using their own name or address does not infringe a registered mark, providing that the use accord with open honest practice.

d) Use of certain indications. The use of certain indications (e.g. the intended purpose of the gods or services or their geographical origin) will not constitute infringement where that use accords with appropriate honest practice.

e) The locality defence. Signs applicable to a certain locality whose use predates the registration of a mark may continue to be used in that locality.

f) Exhaustion. Trademark rights are exhausted once the proprietor has consented to the placing of goods bearing the mark on the market within the EEA. For example, once a brand owner consents to a consignment of their goods being marketed in France, trademark rights cannot be used to prevent these goods from being resold in the UK, unless there are legitimate reasons for this. Goods sold in this way are known as 'grey imports' or parallel imports.

For remedies for infringement please refer to chapter 1.

Now read the key points from chapter 4 overleaf.

Key points from Chapter Four

- A trademark is a symbol or a sign placed on, or used in relation to, one trader's goods or services to distinguish them from similar goods or services supplied by other trader.

- The Trademarks Act 1994 is the main legislation covering trademarks.

- There are a number of international conventions and arrangements that give some international recognition to national trademarks.

- An application for a national trademark may be made to the Trademarks registry. Community trademarks, which cover the European Union, can be made through the Community Trademarks Office.

5

Passing Off

·····

In the last chapter we examined trademarks. In this chapter we will look at what is known as 'passing off. In particular we will look at the following areas:

·····

- Definition of passing off
- The differences between infringement and passing off
- The requirements of a passing off action
- Misrepresentation
- Confusion
- Damage
- Injurious falsehood
- Remedies

·····

.

Passing off

The practice of 'passing off' involves one trader giving the impression that his goods are those of another trader who has an established goodwill. I am sure that we have all seen it, from fast food to sportswear to publications and so on. It also occurs where one trader indicates that his goods are of the same quality as another trader or where one trader creates the impression of association with another trader. Where an existing trader has a reputable or popular good or service, another trader will hope to take commercial advantage of the goodwill that has been built up. The first trader will suffer loss of sales and, subsequently, goodwill and loss if the goods are in any way sub-standard.

Honest traders are protected against these activities by the law of passing off. Passing off is a tort. It provides common law protection of brand names and get-up. This form of action is used either where the mark is an unregistered mark, or where the mark is unregistrable. For registered marks, the proprietor can bring an action for passing off as well as trade mark infringement. In court, the issues will be the same namely, there must be a balance between protecting the proprietor's goodwill, while protecting the interests of other legitimate traders. The interests of other consumers must also be considered.

The difference between infringing trademarks and passing off
Once a trademark has been registered, protection against infringement is automatic. Trademarks are a form of personal property and their use by another without permission constitutes interference with that person's property right. On the other hand, the claimant in a passing off action must demonstrate the presence of goodwill in order to have a right of action. The common law protects the goodwill of a business associated with a trade name or get-up, while trademark legislation protects rights in the actual name. The protection provided in passing off is potentially broader. Business goodwill can cover the name of the goods or services in question, business methods, get-up and marketing style.

Two cases sum up the difference in protection provided. In Coca-Cola Trademark Applications (1986) the House of Lords refused to allow the registration of the shape of the famous bottle, because it was concerned about the creation of a monopoly. In

Reckitt and Coleman Products Ltd v Bordern Inc (1990) the same court restrained the defendants use of a plastic container resembling the defendants lemon in a passing off action. Registration of shapes, as discussed, is now allowed under the 1994 Trademarks Act.

The traditional form of passing off is where the defendant gives the consumer the impression that the goods sold are actually those of the claimant. A defendant may also be found to be passing off one quality of the claimant's goods as goods of another quality. In A.G. Spalding and Bros v A.W. Gammage Ltd (1915) the claimants manufactured 'Orb' footballs. They applied their mark to two types of ball, and sold the inferior type to waste rubber merchants. The defendant bought those inferior products and sold then in such a way as to imply that they were the higher quality 'orb' footballs. This was a clear case of passing off and was held to be so.

However, once a defendant has established goodwill in his own product using the claimant's name, it becomes very difficult to restrain him. In Vine Products Ltd v Mackenzie Ltd (1969) Spanish producers of sherry tried to stop the use of the name sherry on products from regions other than Jerez in Spain. However, in this case, producers in other countries and regions were able to show that they had already established goodwill in their sherry. As a result of this, the courts established that they were able to continue with the use of the name sherry, with the country of origin as a prefix.

The requirements of a passing off action

The minimum requirements for a successful action in passing off were laid down by Lord Diplock in Erven Warnink Besloven Vennootschap v J Townsend and Sons Ltd (1979). These were:

'(1) a misrepresentation (2) made by a trader in the course of trade (3) to prospective customers of his or ultimate customers of goods or services supplied by him, (4) which is calculated to injure the business or goodwill of another trader (in the sense that it is a reasonably foreseeable consequence) and (5) which causes actual damage to the business or goodwill of the trader by whom the action is brought will probably do so'

These five requirements were reduced to three by Reckitt and Coleman products v Bordern Ltd (1990) as: (a) the existence of claimants goodwill (b) a misrepresentation and (c) damage or likely damage to the claimants goodwill or reputation.

The claimant's goodwill

The claimant must establish goodwill associated with goods or their get-up. Goodwill has been defined as: 'the whole advantage, whatever it may be, of the reputation and connection of the firm which have been built up by the years of honest work or gained by lavish expenditure of money'. Trego v Hunt (1895). This interpretation has stood the test of time. Reputation is built up over time and customers develop loyalty and recognition of a product's inherent worth.

Goodwill can be localised. One business, say in Liverpool cannot really stop another business in Sussex using a name if it is local to a business, such as 'Cutters' hairdressing. However, if the business has a national or international reputation then this is a different matter.

Misrepresentation

The misrepresentation need not be intentional for a passing off action to succeed and innocence of misrepresentation is no defence. However, the defendant's state of mind may influence the remedy awarded by a court. The misrepresentation may be in respect of the origin of the goods, their quality or even the way in which they are made. Most of the cases of misrepresentation concern origin and quality. In Coombes International v Scholl (1977) the claimant manufactured insoles called 'Odor eaters' which contained activated charcoal. The defendant, who was a well-known manufacturer of footwear, also produced odour eaters. These were packaged in the same way. An injunction was granted on the basis that there was a misrepresentation as to the origins of the defendant's products, which was found to be inferior.

Misrepresentation and confusion

Confusion is by degree and the claimant in such a case would need evidence that the confusion is significant enough for an action to be brought. Several well known cases highlight this. Neutrogena Corp and Another v Golden Ltd and Another (1996). The claimants sold a range of hypo-allergic products for the skin and hair under the name Neutrogena. The defendants started marketing a similar, but narrower range of skin and hair products under the name Neutralia. The claimants argued that use of the prefix 'Neutr' lead to confusion. Varied evidence of confusion was demonstrated. This included complaints about a Neutralia advertisement, which the complainants had taken to be for Neutrogena. Other evidence was produced, of a substantial nature and the courts held that the legal test on the issue of deception was whether, on a balance of probabilities, a substantial number of members of the public would be misled into purchasing the defendants product in the belief that it was the claimant's. the court felt that the evidence produced demonstrated confusion caused by the defendants' mark.

Confusion and common fields of activity

Traditionally, there was a need for the claimant and defendant to be in the same field of business activity before it was considered likely that there would be confusion leading to injury and goodwill. This qualification has prevented some individuals from stopping the unauthorised use of their name. In McCulloch v May (1947) the claimant was a well-known children's broadcaster who used the name 'Uncle Mac'. The defendant sold cereal under the name 'Uncle Mac' alluding to some of the claimant's characteristics, without his permission. The claimant failed in his action for passing off as he was not involved in the making or marketing of cereals. According to the court, there had to be a common field of activity in which, however remotely, the claimant and defendant were engaged.

The need for a common field of activity to be established before action can be taken has had a detrimental effect on the commercial practice of character merchandising. This is where the names or pictures of famous characters, whether real or fictional, are applied to everyday goods to make them more marketable.

In Lynstad v Anabus Products Ltd (1977) the members of the group ABBA were unable to stop their pictures being applied to T shirts because they were in the entertainment business and not in the same field of manufacturers of clothing. However, there is a general move away from this rigid approach to character merchandising which will be discussed further on.

Damage

The claimant must show damage or a probability of damage. The damage need not be tangible. A claimant can employ a range of methods to prove confusion leading to lost sales or dilution of reputation. One method is the use of surveys although this is not seen as a reliable way of providing evidence. If surveys are used they should be properly carried out otherwise the results may be discredited by the courts. Therefore, good statistical methods should be employed.

Domain names

Domain names are the internet addresses registered by users of the internet. They perform similar functions to trademarks. However, the domain name system is far less flexible than that for registration of trademarks. Each name given is unique so that there is little scope for other businesses to use it. The courts, when dealing with domain names have shown a willingness to allow actions for passing off and trademark infringement under s.10 (3).

One case, British Telecommunications Plc v One in a Million Ltd and Other's (1999) the defendant had registered a large number of domain names comprising the names or trade marks of well known businesses without asking permission. None were in use as active websites. The defendants had registered them with a view to selling them to the owners of the goodwill or collectors. Among the brands concerned were Marks and Spencers, Sainsbury, Ladbrokes, Virgin and British Telecom.

These companies sued the defendants alleging passing off and trademark infringement. In Marks and Spencer's case the Court of Appeal were of the opinion that the use of the name in a domain created the impression that the defendants were somehow involved or linked to Marks and Spencer. Although the other cases were slightly different the Court of Appeal held in favour of the claimants and infringement was upheld.

Injurious falsehood

In between the torts of defamation and passing off there is injurious falsehood. The action is also referred to as malicious. It is linked to passing off because it is another form of protection for a trader's goodwill. It is also defamation because the defendant has, allegedly, libelled the business of another trader. To succeed, the claimant must show that the defendant maliciously made false statements about the claimant's goods or services, which were calculated to cause damage. If the defendant's statements about the claimant's goods is true, there is no action, the onus is on the claimant to prove that the statement is false.

Remedies

Damages are available in a passing off action. These are usually based on the actual loss suffered as far as that can be calculated. Damages may also be calculated on a royalty basis, in other word the amount that the defendant would have paid if he had applied for a licence to use the claimant's name or mark. It is also the norm to obtain an injunction to restrain defendants activities.

Now read the key points from chapter 5 overleaf.

Key points from Chapter Five

- The process of passing off involves one trader giving the impression that his goods or services are the same as, or associated with, another trader's.

- The claimant in a passing off action must demonstrate the presence of goodwill in order to have the right of action.

- The misrepresentation need not be intentional for a passing off action to succeed.

- Traditionally, there has been the need for the claimant and defendant to be in the same are of business before it can be considered that a confusion leading to injury and loss of goodwill can arise.

- The law has developed to enable those who bring passing off actions to obtain relief without having to prove the same field of activity.

6

Character Merchandising

···

In the last chapter we looked at the practice of passing off. In this chapter we will look specifically at the area of character merchandising, looking particularly at the following areas:

···
.

- Definition of character merchandising
- Character merchandising and defamation
- Character merchandising and copyright
- Character merchandising and registered trade marks
- Character merchandising and passing off

···

Character merchandising

Character merchandising is a very significant business activity amounting to many millions of pounds. It is, essentially, the practice of using the name and/or image of a popular character, whether real or fictional, to promote products.

The way character merchandising should work is that an organisation specialising in merchandising will obtain a licence from the creator of the character which allows for the representation of that character on a certain product, in return for a licence fee. Some traders will avoid paying a fee and will use the character anyway and can sell their goods at a lower price than a licensed trader. In addition, quality becomes an issue, as unlicensed traders will not have to conform to any standard.

The legal protection against unauthorised use of characters is not very clear. In passing off, protection has been hampered by the need to establish a common field of activity between the owner of the character and the person using it.

Character merchandising and defamation

In certain cases, an actual person can stop unauthorised use of their character by suing for defamation. An example of an action of this sort is Tolley v Fry (1931). The claimant was an amateur golfer. His picture was used by the defendants to advertise their chocolate without consent. They were subsequently sued for libel. The claimant successfully claimed that anyone using his picture would think that he had compromised his amateur status by accepting money for advertising. Tolley succeeded because it was held that 'the defendants had published a false statement which lowered him in the estimation of right thinking members of society'. The advertisement suggested that he had compromised his amateur status and so fell within the standard definition of defamation.

Defamation, however, is only a viable course of action if a name has been used to promote something undesirable.

Character merchandising and copyright

Copyright offers some protection. Section 1 (1)(a) of the Copyrights, Designs and Patents Act 1988, states that copyright subsists in 'original literary, dramatic, musical or artistic works'. The owners of a character can protect its image, under the Act as an artistic work. Under s.4, photographs and drawings are included as artistic works. Anybody making a copy of the work, or issuing copies of it to the public without the copyright owner's permission, is guilty of infringement according to ss..17-18. So putting an unauthorised copy of a cartoon on a T-shirt would amount to an infringement, as would selling the T-shirt bearing a copy of that cartoon.

Copyright does have its limitations. There are difficulties where only the name of a character is used, as there is no copyright or titles, no matter how distinctive. Even if a picture of a character is used, the copyright owner must show that the representation is an exact or substantial copy, as copyright protects the expression of an idea and not the idea itself. Where the representation is a photograph of a real personality, the personality will only be able to use copyright to protect his image if the copyright in the photograph has been assigned to him, as, since 1st August 1988, the copyright in a photograph usually belongs to the person taking it.

A case highlighting an attempt to use copyright to protect a personality's features, is the case of Merchandising Corp of America v Harpbond (1983). This case concerned the group Adam and the Ants and in particular the distinctive face make up worn by the lead singer. The claimant sued the defendants for reproducing the pictures of Adam Ant with his distinctive make up claiming that the make up was a copyright work (a painting). This argument was rejected by the court

Character merchandising and registered trademarks
Since the passing of the 1994 Trademarks Act, personalities can apply to register their names, caricatures and any other identifying mark. Examples of trademarks that have been applied for or registered are Paul Gascoigne's application to register a caricature of himself and also the name 'Shearer' and the number 9 shirt.

Character merchandising and passing off

The use of passing off as a form of protection has been hindered by the notion of 'common field of activity'. In Wombles Ltd v Wombles Skips (1977) the case concerned the Wombles who were fictitious characters well known for clearing up litter. The defendants formed a company to hire out skips, and used the name 'Wombles' because of the connection to tidiness. The claimant claimed a common field of activity in their claim as the Wombles had granted a licence to reproduce the Wombles on wastepaper baskets. The case failed because the courts held that there was no common field of activity.

Another important case was that of Taverner Rutledge v Trexapalm Ltd (1977) concerning the TV character Kojak, famous for sucking lollipops. The claimant made lollipops similar in shape to those used by Kojak and sold them as 'Kojakpops'. It quickly established goodwill in the name for the products, yet did not have, and had not sought a licence from the TV company responsible for the series. The defendants, who obtained a licence from the company created lollipops, called Kojak lollies. The claimants sued for passing off. Although it was argued that the defendants licence, with quality control terms illustrated a connection in the course of business and the owners of the name, in other words a common field of activity, this argument failed because there was no actual or potential common field of activity between the owners of the television series and the defendants business, there being no evidence of the exercise of quality control by the owners of the series.

According to the Judge, the defendant would have to show that the practice of character merchandising had become so well know that as soon as anybody in the street realised that a product was licensed by the owners of some series, like Kojak, he would say to himself not only 'this must have been licensed by them' but also ' and that is a guarantee of its quality'. In this case, the claimant's lollies were of better value and quality than the defendant's product, which would have harmed the claimant's reputation.

The reference to quality control is important in that it indicates a way to get around the problems of common field of activity. Stricter quality control exercised through the terms of a licence should indicate an active interest in the type of goods being produced and thereby form the necessary connection in the course of trade.

The case involving Mirage Studios v Counter Feat Clothing Co Ltd (1991) illustrates recognition that the public are well aware of the practice of character merchandising. The claimants created the 'Teenage Mutant Ninja Turtle' characters. They also made and marketed cartoons, films and videos containing these characters. Part of the claimants business involved licensing the reproduction of the images. Without the claimant's permission the defendant made drawings, similar to the Ninja Turtles but not exact reproductions and licensed the use of these.

The courts granted an injunction against the defendants stating that a misrepresentation had taken place because there was evidence to show that a substantial number of the buying public expected, and knew, where a famous cartoon or television character was reproduced on goods, that reproduction was the result of a licence granted by the owner of the copyright or owner of other rights nib the character. It was held:

' Since the public associated the goods with the creator of the characters, the depreciation of the image by fixing the Turtles picture to inferior goods and inferior material might seriously reduce the value of the licensing rights'. This decision has been generally welcomed and should help somewhat to clear up problems associated with the notion of 'common field of activity'.

Now read the key points from chapter 6 overleaf.

Key points from Chapter Six

- Character merchandising is the practice of using the name and/or image of a popular character, whether real or fictional, to promote a product.

- The legal protection against unauthorised use of these characters is not very clear and is hampered by the need to establish a common field of practice.

- The law of copyright offers some protection, but this is limited.

- Characters and personalities can register as trademarks in order to provide protection.

7

Copyright

....

In the last chapter we looked at the area of character merchandising. In this chapter we look specifically at the area of copyright, in particular the following areas:

....

- Definition of copyright
- Historical background
- Subsistence of copyright
- Copyright works
- Dramatic works
- Musical works
- Artistic works
- Sound recordings
- Film
- Broadcasts
- The typography right
- Originality
- Fixation and tangibility
- Copyright and the employee
- Establishing authorship
- Duration of copyright

....

Definition of copyright

The Copyright, Designs and Patents Act 1988 is the principle piece of legislation governing copyright. This was amended by the Copyright and Related Rights Regulations 2003, which transposed Directive 2001/29/EC and harmonised certain aspects of copyright law and related rights. However, for the purposes of this book it is the 1988 Act that we will refer to.

Copyright is the right to prevent others copying or reproducing an individuals or other's work. *Copyright protects the expression of an idea and not the idea itself.* Only when an idea is committed to paper can it be protected. Others can be directly or indirectly stopped from copying the whole or a substantial part of a copyright work. However, others cannot be stopped from borrowing an idea or producing something very similar.

Copyright is a right that arises automatically upon the creation of a work that qualifies for copyright protection. This means that there is no registration certificate to prove ownership. To claim ownership the author will have to produce original and preferably dated evidence of the creation of the work and proof of authorship. The author will also need to show that he is a qualifying person and that the work was produced in a convention country.

To be a qualifying person (s.154 of the Copyright Designs and Patents Act 1988) the author must have been, at the material time, a British Citizen, subject or protected person, a British Dependant territories citizen, a British nationals (overseas) or a British Overseas Citizen or must have been resident or domiciled in a convention country at the material time, which is when the work was first published. If the author dies before publication the material time is before his death.

A convention country is a country that is signatory to the Universal Copyright Convention or the Berne Copyright Convention, which includes most countries in the world.

The works that can qualify for protection are defined in S.1 of the 1988 Act. These are:

a) Original literary, dramatic, musical and artistic works
b) Sound recordings, films, broadcasts and cable programmes
c) Typographical arrangements of published editions

Duration of copyright

The 1988 Copyright, Designs and Patents Act states duration as:

1. For literary, dramatic, musical or artistic works-70 years from the end of the calendar year in which the last remaining author of the work dies. If the author is unknown, copyright will last for 70 years from the end of the calendar year in which the work was created, although if it is made available to the public during that time then the duration will be 70 years from the end of the year that the work was first made available.

2. Sound recordings and broadcasts-50 years from the end of the calendar year in which the work was created, or if the work was released within that time 50 years from the end of the calendar year in which the work was released.

3. Films-70 years from the end of the calendar year in which the last principal director, author or composer dies. If the work is of unknown authorship, 70 years from the end of

the calendar year of creation or 70 years at the end of the year that the work was first made available.

4. Typographical arrangement of published editions-25 years from the end of the calendar year in which the work was first published.

5. Broadcasts and cable programmes-50 years from the end of the year in which the broadcast was made.

Historical background

Copyright has its origins in the 16th century. The courts recognised a need for some form of protection for books. In 1556, a system of registration of books was established to offer protection for authors. If an author registered a book with the Stationers Company it gave him/her a perpetual right to reproduce the book and prevent reproduction by anyone else. For almost 200 years this form of protection only applied to books. In 1734 this extended to engravings (Engravings Copyright Act) A number of Acts were passed over the next 150 years extending copyright protection to musical, dramatic and artistic works. In 1875, a Royal Commission was set up to look at the position and recommended a clear approach be adopted to copyright protection, codified into one single Act. This happened after Great Britain signed the Berne Copyright Convention in 1885.

The Berne Convention provided for international protection of copyright for the work of all nationals of all countries signing the convention. It also required each member country to extend minimum standards of protection to nationals of all other member countries.

The United Kingdom implemented the 1911 Copyright Act to put into place minimum standards and also draw together previous legislation. The next Act, prompted by changes in the Berne Convention led to the 1956 Copyright Act This Act reflected changes, amongst other things, in the field of technology.

In 1973, the Whitford Committee was appointed to review the state of copyright law. The Committee reported in 1977 suggesting numerous changes to the law, resulting in a Green paper in 1981, 'Reform of the law relating to Copyright, Designs and Performers Protection' and subsequently the White Paper 'Intellectual Property and Innovation' which led to the 1988 Copyright Designs and Patents Act, which was a consolidating Act. Since the Act came into force in August 1989, there have been a number of amending regulations dealing with implementation of EC Directives on rights to reproduce copyright software as is necessary for lawful use, protection of semiconductor chip topography rights and harmonisation of copyright duration. There are further legislative moves afoot to update copyright law to deal with the growth of new technology.

Copyright – subsistence of copyright

As shown above, copyright is a property right that subsists in certain works. It is a statutory right giving the copyright owner certain exclusive rights in relation to his or her work. In the 1988 Copyright Designs and Patents act there are nine categories of copyright works:

'Authorial' 'Primary' or 'LDMA' works

1) Literary works
2) Dramatic works
3) Musical works

4) Artistic works

'Entrepreneurial' 'Secondary' or 'Derivative' works

5) Sound recordings
6) Films
7) Broadcasts
8) Cable programmes
9) Typographical arrangements of published editions (the typography right)

Copyright comes into existence, or subsists automatically where a qualifying person creates a work that is original and tangible (or fixed).

Qualification

Copyright will not subsist in a work unless:

a) It has been created by a qualifying person
b) It was first published in a qualifying country
c) In the case of literary, dramatic and musical works, the work must be fixed, that is reduced to a material form in writing or otherwise.

Copyright works

The CDPA 1988 defines a literary work as being 'any work written, spoken or sung, other than a dramatic or musical work'. A novel or poem could equally fall into this category. Additionally, the concept of literary works extends to tables (e.g. a rail timetable) compilations such as directories and computer programmes. Databases are also regarded as literary works. In essence, any work that can be expresses in print, irrespective of quality, will be a literary work.

Dramatic works

The CDPA 1988 defines 'dramatic works' as including works of dance or mime. In the case Norowzian v Arks (1999) it was stated that these terms should be given their natural and ordinary meaning, the implication being that dramatic works are works of *action*. The courts also recognised in this case that films may be produced as dramatic works, either as dramatic works in themselves and/or as a recording of a dramatic work.

Musical works

A musical work is a work consisting solely of musical notes, any words or actions intended to be sung, spoken or recorded with the notes are excluded. Therefore, a melody is a musical works with the lyrics being literary.

Artistic works

A wide-ranging definition of artistic works is provided by the CDPA 1988 s.4. Works of architecture are included but focus is usually placed on the remaining artistic works. These fall into two categories:

a) Works protected irrespective of their artistic merit:

    i)   Graphic works, i.e. paintings, drawings, diagrams, maps, charts, plans, engravings, etchings, lithographs, woodcuts or similar works

    ii)   Photographs

    iii)   Sculptures. The protection of functional objects, such as a cast is problematic. In one notable case in New Zealand Wham-O manufacturing Co v Lincoln Industries Ltd (1985) a wooden model of a Frisbee was held to be a sculpture. The modern UK position is almost certainly more restrictive, as objects will not now be protected as sculptures where they are not made for the purpose of sculpture.

iv) Collages. Collages are artistic or functional visual arrangements produced by affixing two or more items together. Intrinsically ephemeral arrangements (for example the composition of a photograph) are not collages.

b) Artistic works required to be of a certain quality (CDPA 1988 s.4 (1) c i.e. works of artistic craftsmanship. Few works can meet the standard of artistic craftsmanship, as they must be both of artistic quality and the result of craftsmanship. These principles were further developed into a two-part test for artistic craftsmanship in Merlet v Mothercare (1986). First, did the creation of the work involve craftsmanship in the sense that skill and pride was invested in its manufacturer? Second, does the work have aesthetic appeal and did an artist create it?

Sound recordings

A sound recording is a reproducible recording of either:

1) Sounds where there is no underlying copyright work (e.g. birdsong)
2) A recording of the whole or any part of a literary, dramatic or musical work.

The format of recording is of no relevance.

Film

The CDPA 1988 s.5B (1) provides that a film is a reproducible recording of a moving image on any medium. It is the recording itself that is protected, rather than the subject matter that has been recorded, but it should be borne in mind that a film might also be protected as a dramatic work. Film soundtracks are taken to be part of the film itself.

Broadcasts

Copyright subsists in sounds and visual images that are broadcast CDPA 1988 s.6 (1), a broadcast being defined as a transmission by wireless telegraphy of visual images, sounds or other information. The definition of 'broadcast' therefore encompasses radio and television broadcasts and both terrestrial and satellite broadcasting.

Cable programmes

The transmission of an item that forms part of a cable programme will create separate works that are capable of protection as cable programmes CDPA 1988 s.7. A cable programme service is defined as a service consisting wholly or mainly in sending visual images, sounds or other information via a telecommunications system which may utilise wires or microwave transmission. Items sent via wireless telegraphy are specifically excluded as they are already protected as broadcasts. This means that as well as subscription channels a website on the internet may be a cable programme service.

The typography right

The CDPA 1988 s.8 affords protection to the typography, that is the layout, of published editions of literary, dramatic and musical works. The leading authority on typographical arrangement copyright is Newspaper Licensing Agency Ltd v Marks and Spencer Plc (2001).

Copyright works the ideas/expression dichotomy

There is no copyright in ideas. Copyright subsists in the tangible expression of ideas and not the ideas themselves. In America this is referred to as the ideas/expression dichotomy. This principle can be helpful but should not be taken too literally, as whilst it is clear that mere ideas cannot be protected by copyright the following points should be noted:

1) What might be termed 'highly developed ideas', for example an early draft of a textbook, would be protected by copyright, as are preparatory design material for computer programmes.
2) Copyright cannot be circumvented by selectively altering the expression of a copyright work in the process of reproducing it.

Originality

The CDPA 1988 s.1 requires that literary, dramatic, musical and artistic works be 'original'. The originality requirements only apply to LDMA works, there is no such requirement for secondary copyright works, although it is clear that no copyright will subsist in secondary copyright works that merely reproduce secondary works.

LDMA works must be original in the sense that they originate with the author. One such case that highlights this is University of London Press v University Tutorial Press (1916). This is a minimal qualitative requirement: original works need not be inventive or original and a wide range of works have been held to be original, from coupons for football pools (Ladbrokes v

William Hill (1964) to a compilation of broadcasting programmes (Independent Television Publications Ltd and the BBC v Time Out Ltd (1984).

Expending skill and judgement in creating an LDMA work usually suffices to deem the work original. Mere copying cannot confer originality. Alternatively, the mere expenditure of effort or labour (the so-called 'sweat of the brow' test for originality) has sometimes been said to be sufficient to confer originality. But in practice some minimum element of originality is required. For example, in Crump v Smythson (1944) it was held that the generic nature of commonplace diary material left no room for judgement in selection and arrangement therefore the resultant works were not original. Originality has also been held to be more than 'competent draftsmanship' (Interlego v Tyon 1988). Commonly databases and computer programmes were the subject matter of sweat of the brow concerns.

Higher standards of originality: computer programs and databases

As a result of two European Directives, The Directive on the Legal Protection of Databases (Directive 96/9/EC) and the Computer Directive (Directive 91/250/EEC) both computer programmes and databases must be original in the sense that they are the author's own intellectual creation. This is a higher standard or originality than that of 'skills, labour and judgement'.

Originality and the *de minimis principle*

The question arises, does copyright exist in very short works. The case, Exxon Corporation v Exxon Ind (1982), where the invented word Exxon was denied copyright protection, is often cited to support the proposition that a de minimis principle applies in copyright law, i.e. that some things are too small to be deemed copyright works. However, the authority for this is not so clear.

Fixation and tangibility

As we have seen, copyright does not subsist in literary, dramatic or musical works until they are recorded in writing or otherwise. This pragmatic requirement is known as 'fixation'. Usually, such works will be fixed by the author, but fixation by a third party (with or without the authors permission is also possible.

Other copyright works are not subject to the fixation requirement. This is usually unproblematic as films, sound recordings, broadcasts, cable programmes and typography are inherently tangible works.

Ownership of copyright and the employee

The rule is that the first owner of copyright in a work is the person who created the work, i.e. the author. A major exception to this rule is CDPA 1988 s.11 (2). Which provides that where a person creates an LDMA work in the course of employment the employer is the first owner of any copyright in the work subject to any agreement to the contrary. There are special provisions for Crown use, Parliamentary copyright and copyright for certain international organisations (CDPA 1988 s.11 (3).

Establishing Authorship

The author is the person who creates the work. Identifying the author is usually a straightforward task. The following is the standard authorship position:

- Literary work. The writer
- Dramatic work. The writer
- Musical work. The composer

- Artistic work. The artist
- Computer generated LDMA works. The person operating the computer.
- Sound recordings. The producer.
- Films. The producer and principal director.
- Broadcasts. The broadcaster.
- Cable programmes. The cable program service provider.
- Typography right. The publisher.
- Any work where the identity of the author is unknown. A work of unknown authorship.

Joint authorship

Where more than one person is involved in the creation of a work, careful consideration is needed in determining individual contributions. A person who suggests a subject to a poet is not the author of the poem. Merely supplying ideas is insufficient for joint authorship; an integral role in the expression of ideas is required. Joint authorship arises where the efforts of the two authors is indistinguishable.

Copyright notices

When establishing authorship, it is important to ensure a copyright notice is clearly evident, obvious and legible and, if applicable the notice should appear on every page. The notice should take the form of:

- The actual term copyright
- The copyright symbol ©
- The year-normally when first published
- The name of the owner, this can be individual, collective or organisation

- For sound recordings there should also be included a phonogram rights notice for the sound recording itself, using the phonogram symbol (p)

Now read the key points from chapter 7 overleaf.

Key points from Chapter Seven

- Copyright is the right to prevent others copying or generally reproducing an individual's or others work.

- The main legislation dealing with copyright is the 1988 Copyright, Designs and Patents Act.

- When an idea is committed to paper it can be protected as copyright. Copyright protects the expression of an idea and not the idea itself.

- Copyright is a right that arises automatically upon the creation of a work that qualifies for copyright protection.

- The Copyright, Design and Patents Act 1988 requires that the Literary, Dramatic, Musical or Artistic work be original, in the sense that they originate with the author.

8

Infringement of Copyright

···

In the last chapter, we looked at copyright. In this chapter, we will look specifically at infringement of copyright, looking particularly at the following areas:

···
.

- Definition of infringement
- Copying works
- Adaptation of works
- Remedies
- Defences to infringement

···
.

Infringement

The owner of copyright has the exclusive right to do certain specified things with the work and the right to grant licences to others or to take action for infringement. The acts, which the owner can do in respect of the work, are copying, issuing copies, performing or showing the work or performing in public or broadcasting the work. An adaptation is also protected as a copyright work.

The restricted acts will only be seen as infringed if the infringement is in relation to the whole or a substantial part of the work. Many infringement cases do indeed involve the reproduction of a substantial part of a work as opposed to the whole. Even if a defendant has built on the part of the copyright infringement and created a new work infringement still exists. There is no general test and each case is different.

If part of the claimant's work is itself an infringement of someone else's copyright that part will be disregarded in any infringement action.

It is an infringement if one person authorises another to do an infringement act. A well known case illustrating this point is Moorhouse v University of New South Wales (1976), where photocopying machines were available in the university library for use by students and other library users. One particular person made two copies of a story from the claimant's book. The decision hinged on whether or not it could be said that the university authorised students to copy literary works without licence and whether, in this case, the university authorised infringement. It was held that Notices around the library and in guides were held not to be enough, as they did not provide clear or adequate warning.

Copying works

This applies to all types of copyright work. In relation to Literary, artistic, dramatic and musical works this means reproduction in any form, whether mechanical or electronic. However, for example, to make a recipe from a recipe book is not seen as reproduction as the person reading is utilising information that the author wishes to share. Artistic works may be infringed by reproducing a two-dimensional work in three dimensions and vice versa (s.17. (3) Of the 1988 CDPA). In the case of architect's plans, it would be an infringement to copy a plan or by building the actual building in the plan. However, it would not be an infringement to make a graphic two-dimensional work (drawing or photo) of a building or of a sculpture, model for a building or work of artistic craftsmanship in a public place because s.62 of the Act specifically says so.

Copying films, broadcasts and cable programmes is said by the 1988 Act as to include photographing any image in the film, broadcast or programme. Copying a typographic arrangement of a published edition means making an exact copy of a published edition. For example sending a published edition to someone by fax is not seen as reproduction.

In relation to the idea/expression divide in relation to deciding what is protected by copyright, even where it is obvious that an idea has been copied it does not necessarily constitute infringement unless the form of expression of the idea has also been copied. Determining this can be difficult. In cases relating to infringement of computer programmes, the use of different computer languages makes it more difficult. One such case highlighting this is Ibcos Computers Ltd v Barclays Mercantile Highland Finance Ltd (1994). In this case, the defendant had loaded a copy of the claimants software without permission, this being copyright infringement. Copying was proved by the existence of marked and unexplained similarities between the claimants and the defendant's code. In this case, the judge set out the correct test of copyright infringement in a case of non-literal copying. The court confirmed that, under English copyright law, the test for infringement was:

a) Is there a work?
b) Is it original?
c) Has there been copying?

d) Was this of a substantial part?

This is a simple but effective test that clearly lays out the guidelines for copyright infringement.

All copyright works may be infringed by the issuing of copies to the public. Issuing means putting into circulation copies of a work not previously put into circulation. This means that once a copy of a copyright owners work has legitimately been put out into circulation in any country the owner cannot prevent subsequent circulation of that copy (whether by sale, loan or distribution). However, the copyright owner still has the right to prevent the making of other copies from that one legitimately circulated copy.

Performing and playing of copyright works in public are also acts of infringement if done without licence. It is also an infringement of a copyright work to broadcast it or to include it in a cable programme service.

Adaptation of works
This act of copyright infringement only relates to literary, dramatic and musical works. Adaptation means a translation of a literary or dramatic work, the conversion of a dramatic work into non-dramatic and vice versa and reproduction of a literary or dramatic work in a form whereby the work is conveyed by pictures suitable for inclusion in a book or periodical. Adaptation also relates to conversion of a computer programme from one computer language to another, unless this conversion happens incidentally as a result of running a programme. However, if the programme was translated in the course of running it on a computer, the act of making a transient copy of the programme

(in either language) in the computer's memory would constitute making a copy and would be an infringement if done without the copyright owner permission. As a result of the EC Software Directive, implemented into English law by ss.50 (a)-(c) of the 1988 Act, a lawful acquirer of software has an implied licence to copy to the extent necessary for lawful use of the software.

Remedies

The remedies available to a copyright owner, and also to a licensee, for copyright infringement have been broadened with the introduction of the 2003 Regulations which make it a criminal offence to infringe copyright or performers rights by making a work available to the public in the course of a business or to an extent which prejudicially affects a copyright owner. The owner can also bring a civil action for damages, injunction to deliver up and also a possible criminal prosecution by the local weights and measures authorities for one or more of the criminal offences under the act, or to prompt seizures and fines by Customs and Excise and/or trading standards office pursuant to specific provisions of the act, the Trade Descriptions Act 1968 and the Copyright (Customs) Regulations 1989.

In the case of infringement the claimant may wish to apply for an interlocutory injunction, because the continued reproduction of infringing articles pending a full hearing could put the copyright owner out of business or be prejudicial in some other way.

An exclusive copyright licensee will have the same rights of the copyright owner in respect of an infringement committed after a licensee has been granted. With the exception of an interlocutory injunction, which the exclusive licensee must bring alone all other actions by a licensee must be brought in conjunction with the copyright owner.

In proceedings relating to copyright infringement, there are a number of presumptions laid down by the 1988 Act (in ss27(4) 104, 105 and 106) that allow certain issues to be assumed and that shift the burden of proof to the other party.

Defences to Copyright infringement

There are a number of defences to infringement:

a) Challenge the existence of copyright or the claimant's ownership of copyright.
b) Deny the infringement.
c) Claim to have been entitled, because of permission granted to do the act in question or argue that it is within one of the statutory fair dealing exemptions or by claiming public interest or EC competition rights.

A claim of ignorance of the law will not work as a defence. Ignorance of subsistence of copyright will, however, have a bearing on any damages awarded. In the case of secondary infringement an element of knowledge is required for the infringement to be actionable in the first place. The infringement only occurs if the person knows that what he or she is dealing with is an infringing copyright work.

If the claimant does own copyright in the work that is allegedly infringed, and facts can be proved, the only defences remaining are:

1) that the defendant had permission from the copyright owner to make a copy.

Provided that the defendant in an infringement action can prove that permission was granted, either in writing, orally or, in certain cases, implied, then the claim of infringement will fail.

2) That the act was one of the permitted acts under the 1988 Act.

The 1988 Act contains statutory permissions, or exceptions, to the exclusive rights of the copyright owner. Many of these have come from the results of case decisions over the years that have acknowledged the need for fair exceptions. These permitted acts are categorised in the Act and comprise:

- Research and private study
- Criticism review and news reporting
- Incidental inclusion of copyright material
- Things done for instruction or examination
- Anthologies for educational use
- Playing, showing or performing in an educational establishment
- Recordings by educational establishments
- Reprographic copying by educational establishments
- Libraries and archives
- Public administration
- Lawful users of computer programs and databases
- Designs
- Typefaces
- Works in electronic form

All of the above are categorised in the Act and each case concerning these categories will be on its own merit.

3) That the exercise of the copyright owner's rights to prevent copying would amount to an anti-competitive practice under EC competition law.

4) That the exercise of the copyright owner's rights is against the public interest.

Each one of the above must be proven and each case will be judged on its own merit.

Now read the key points from chapter 8 overleaf.

Key points from Chapter Eight

- The owner of copyright has the exclusive right to do certain specified things with the work and the right to grant licenses to others or take action for infringement.

- An infringement will only occur when the whole or a substantial part of a work has been copied.

- The remedies available to a copyright owner, and also to a licensee, for infringement are those of damages, injunction, delivering up and also possible criminal prosecution.

9

Design

··

In the last chapter, we looked specifically at infringement of rights. In this chapter we will look at design, particularly the following areas:

··

.

- Design and the law
- Protecting design
- The design right
- Ownership of a design
- Rights of the owner of a design
- Secondary infringement
- Exceptions to infringements
- Duration of the design right
- Remedies
- Registered designs
- Novel ideas

··

Design

Designs are protected through a system of registered design rights under the Registered Designs Act 1949, as amended, and design right, with a residual role for copyright, governed by the Copyright, Design and Patents Act 1988.

Traditionally, copyright was an important source of protection in the design field, but a separate system of registered design was developed to protect aesthetic designs. Before the late 1980's, there was a choice of applying for a registered design or relying on copyright, copyright being seen as a stronger form of protection. However, in some cases, copyright was abused in relation to non-aesthetic designs. In British Leyland v Armstrong (1986), the courts were reduced to relying on a non-IP concept, that of non-derogation from grant, to prevent copyright in spare car parts being used to develop a de facto monopoly in such parts.

The end result was a series of reforms in the late 1980's, which saw some reform of registered designs, the cutting back of the role of copyright in the design field and the introduction of a new intellectual property right for design right. More recently, in response to European developments, further reforms were introduced in 2001 to expand the registered design regime.

Protecting a design

A design may be protected by one or more routes:

a) The Copyright, Design and Patents Act 1988 ss.213-264 (Part 111) (The Design Right)
b) Registered Designs (Registered Designs Act 1949, as amended)
c) Copyright (artistic copyright) CDPA 1988 s.51-53.

The design right

The unregistered design right was originally introduced to extend protection to functional designs. Design rights will automatically subsist in both functional and aesthetic designs where there is:

1) A design, any aspect of the design, shape or configuration, internal or external of the whole or part of an article.
2) Qualification of the design
3) Originality (not commonplace in the design field in question at the time of creation
4) The design must be recorded
5) The design is not an excluded design

1) A design

This is defined as 'the design of any aspect of the shape or configuration (internal or external) of the whole or part of an article' (CDPA 1988 s.213) (2). This means that the shape of an article or its configuration may be protected in respect of the whole article or its constituent parts. The features of an article that are protected may be invisible to the human eye.

2) Qualification

The design must qualify for protection via a 'qualifying person' (a person who is a citizen or subject of a qualifying country or a person who is domiciled in a qualifying country). This person could be the designer, the commissioner of the design, the employer of the designer or the first person to market the design.

3) Originality

A design will not be deemed as original if it is commonplace in the design field in question at the time of its creation (CDPA 1988 s.213 (4). The leading case in the field of originality is Farmers Build Ltd v Carrier Bulk Materials Handling Ltd (1999) where it was commented that a design had to be original in the sense that it is the independent work of the designer. In deciding whether the design in question was commonplace, and therefore not original the following was noted:

1) the design must not have been copied from the design of an earlier article.
2) The design should be compared with the design of contemporaneous articles produced by other Parties in the same field. Evidence from experts in the relevant field should be included.
3) This comparison is one of fact and degree. The closer the similarity of the various designs, the more likely that it is that the design is commonplace. However, where aspects of the claimant's design are only to be found on the defendant's design, the court is entitled to conclude that the design in question is not commonplace.

4) **Recorded**

For the design right to subsist, the design must be recorded either as a model or as a design document. Oral disclosure of the design, therefore, would be insufficient.

5) **Exclusions**

The following are excluded from the ambit of the design right:

- Methods or principles of construction
- 'Must fit' designs are excluded. Design rights will not subsist in 'features of shape or configuration of an article which enable the article to be connected to, placed in, around or against, another article so that either article can perform its functions. Hence, design features that allow the article to interface, link, connect or otherwise

physically relate to another article are excluded. Must fit has been held to extend to features of the human body, such as contact lenses.

- 'Must match' designs are excluded, i.e. design rights will not subsist in 'features of shape' or configuration which are dependent upon the appearance of another article of which the article is intended by the designer to form an integral part. Therefore, any features which need to be made in a certain way for aesthetic reasons.

- Surface decoration. Design rights do not exist in surface decoration such as a paint finish or beading on the surface of an article.

The 'must fit' and 'must match' exclusions were primarily intended to limit the registration of spare parts. 'Must fit' related to functional considerations and 'must match' is an aesthetic version of the 'must fit' exclusion.

Ownership of a design

The designer is the first owner of an unregistered design unless:

a) The design was commissioned. The commissioner is the first owner.
b) The design was made in the course of employment. The employer is the first owner.
c) Where the design right subsists via qualification, with reference to the first marketer of the design, that person is the first owner of the design.

Rights of the owner of a design

The owner of a design right has the exclusive right to reproduce the design for commercial purposes. In the context of design rights the CDPA 1988 s.226 (2) requires that copying be proved. It constitutes infringement for any person to engage in the following for commercial purposes without the permission of the design right owner: to copy the design and then produce articles or design documents that are identical or substantially similar to the design.

Secondary infringement
This occurs where, without the permission of the owner, infringing articles are imported or dealt with where that person knows or has reason to believe that an article is infringing.

Exceptions to infringement
There are exceptions to infringement as follows:

a) Where copyright subsists in a work in which a design right also subsists, it is not an infringement of the design right to do anything that constitutes copyright infringement in the work.

b) Any person is entitled to a 'licence of right' in the last five years of the design right (CDPA 1988 s.237)

c) There is a specific provision for Crown use of design (CDPA 1988 s.240).

Duration of design right
The design right subsists from the date upon which the design right is recorded or an article is made to the design (CDPA 1988 s.213(6). Where an article made to the design is sold within five years of the end of the first calendar year from that date, the right will subsist for ten years from the end of the year of first marketing. Otherwise the right endures for fifteen years from the date on which the design is recorded in a design document or in

an article. During the first five years 'licences of right' may be available to third parties.

Registered designs

The registered design's regime underwent substantial reform in December 2001 in order to implement the directive on the Legal protection of Designs (Directive 98/71/EC). The Directive is intended to harmonise the laws of EU member states. The following may be registered under the Registered Design Act 1949, as amended:

a) A 'design' which refers to various aspects of the whole or part of a product.
b) That is novel.
c) That has individual character.
d) Does not fall into any of the exceptions to registration:

- is not a component part of a complex product that is not visible during normal use
- is not a feature solely dictated by technical functions
- is not a 'must fit' design
- is not a design contrary to public policy or the accepted principles of morality.

Since 2001, there has been a big increase in the number of things that are registrable. The introduction of a twelve month grace period and the reform of infringement to the advantage of the owner are other features of the new regime, with the result that registered design protection, previously rather protected and narrow in scope is now an attractive option. The old regime will continue to apply to all registrations and pending applications existing before December 9th 2001 but the new law will apply to the scope of registration and infringement. Hereafter, this chapter refers to the new regime only.

Design

The Registered Design Act 1949 defines a design as 'the appearance of the whole or part of a product resulting from the features of, in particular, the lines, contours, colours, shapes texture or materials of the product or its ornamentation' (RDA 1949 s.1 (2). Any aspect of the appearance of a product are therefore registrable. Aesthetic designs are protected, but functional designs will be protected provided that they are solely dictated by technical function. 'Product' is defined as 'any industrial or handicraft item other than a computer programme. This definition includes get up and packaging and also graphic symbols and typefaces.

Novelty

The RDA 1949 s.1B provides that a design is new if no identical design or those differing only in immaterial details has been made available for the public before the date of the application for the registered design. The novelty rule takes the form of a qualified type of global novelty. A design is novel where, at the application date, it could not have been known to commercial persons in the European Economic Area, specialising in the relevant sector. This is subject to a twelve-month grace period.

Individual character

In addition to novelty, a design must have individual character (RDA 1949 s 1B). A design will be considered to have individual character if 'the overall impression it produces on the informed user differs from the overall impression produced on a user by an earlier design' (RDA 1949 s.1B (3). In assessing whether the design has this quality, the degree of freedom of the designer in developing the design is to be taken into consideration.

There are exceptions to registration as follows:

a) Component part(s) of a complex product that are not visible during normal use may not be registered. 'Complex product' is defined as 'a product composed of at least two replaceable parts permitting the disassembly and re-assembly of the product.

b) Features that are solely dictated by technical functions are not registrable.

c) 'Must fit' designs are not registrable.

d) Designs contrary to public policy or accepted standards of morality are not acceptable.

Ownership

The designer is the first owner of a registered design, unless the design was commissioned or created in the course of employment.

Cancellation of registrations

A registered design may be cancelled by the registrar upon the successful application for a declaration of invalidity (RDA 1949 s.11). Any person may make an application for an application for a declaration of invalidity, the grounds including

- that the design does not satisfy one or more of the requirements of the RDA 1949, i.e. there is not a novel design with individual character, or it is a design dictated by technical function, a 'must fit design' or a design contrary to public policy or morality.

- it is a design excluded by RDA 1949, schedule A1 (the utilisation of devices or symbols connected to the Olympics or royalty)
- It is caught by the provisions of prior trademark rights or copyright.

Rights of the registered design owner

The proprietor of a registered design has the exclusive right to use the design, or any design, which does not produce on the informal user a different impression, i.e. any product incorporating a registered design may infringe the registration.

Infringement

Once granted, protection begins on the filing date and is renewable every five years up to twenty-five years (RDA 1949 s.8).

A registered design will be infringed where a person carries out any of the rights exclusive to the registered proprietor, there are exceptions to infringement including:

a) Private and non commercial use of the design
b) Experimental use of the design
c) Reproducing the design for teaching purposes, with some qualifications.
d) There are some specific exclusions relating to ships or aircraft registered in a third country but temporarily in the UK.
e) Exhaustion within the EEA.
f) Certain acts relating to spare parts.
g) No proceedings may be brought for acts committed before the grant of certificate of registration.
h) Crown use of the design.

Remedies

For design right infringement, the following remedies are available:

1) Damages. Damages are not available against an innocent primary infringer and against the innocent secondary infringer.

2) Injunctions

3) Account of profits

4) An order for delivery up

5) An order for disposal

6) There is a provision for groundless threat of infringement proceedings.

Artistic copyright

In effect, only original design articles and design documents may only be protected by copyright law as artistic works. The CDPA 1988 ss51-52 limits the role of copyright in the design field. Copyright will not subsist in the following:

a) Articles and design documents other than artistic works.

b) Where an article is made to the copy/ design article made from design

The duration of copyright in the design field is as follows:

a) Life of the author plus 70 years

b) Where the design is applied industrially (more than 50 copies made) the copyright term in the industrial design field is limited to 25 years from the date of first marketing. Some things are excluded from this such as sculptures, medals and printed matter of primarily an artistic or literary character.

Now read the key points from chapter 9 overleaf.

Key points from Chapter Nine

- Designs are registered through a system of registered design rights under the Registered Design Act 1949, as amended in 2001, with a residual role for the Copyright, Design and Patents act 1988.

- The designer is the first owner of a registered design unless the design was commissioned, the design was made in the course of employment and where the design rights subsist, via qualification, with reference to the first marketer of the design.

- There are a number of remedies available for infringement such as damages, injunctions and account of profits.

10

Intellectual Property and Information Technology

....

Finally:

A brief look at protection of software, databases and computer programmes generally.

Patenting computer software

Programs for computers can be patented if they produce an 'technical effect'. If a program does not produce a technical effect when run on a computer it is unlikely to be patentable. A technical effect is an improvement in technology and needs to be in an area of technology which is patentable.

Key examples are an improved program for translating between one language and another will not be patentable because linguistics is a mental process whereas a program which speeds up image enhancement may be patentable because it produces a technical improvement in a technical area.

The European Patent Office takes a similar approach to the UK patent Office on patenting software. Deciding whether or not a particular computer program is patentable is a complex issue and advice from either a patent agent or from the UK Patent Office website which has a practice note on patenting software.

Domain names

A domain name works like a company name and is a name by which a company or organization is known on the internet. A more detailed explanation of domain names is contained on the Institute of Trade mark Attorneys web site. In particular, see the press release 'Securing your trade mark from cybersquatters'

If you have a registered trade mark, it is not automatically the case that it can be used as a domain name because the same mark may be registered by different proprietors for different goods and services. If you have a query in this area you should seek advice from Nominet UK, who also offer a dispute resolution service. Nominet UK is the national registry for all domain names ending in 'uk'. To register a domain name ending in 'uk' you must apply to Nominet UK.

Database rights

A database, which is a collection of data, or other material that is arranged in a way which makes individual items accessible, may be protected by copyright or a database right. For copyright protection to apply to a database, the database must have originality in the selection or arrangement of the contents. For database right to apply, the database must be the end result of a significant investment. Databases can satisfy both requirements so that both database right and copyright can apply.

Database right is similar to copyright. There is no registration for database right-it is an automatic right, like copyright and commences as soon as the material that can be protected exists in a recorded form. Database right can apply to either paper or electronic bases. There are, however, differences between database rights and copyright:

- Database protection is much shorter than copyright-15 years from making but, if published during this time, 15 years from being published
- The activities that a right holder can control are a bit different. Database right concerns control over the extraction and re-utilisation of the contents of the database
- The exceptions to the right, activities that the user can undertake without the right holder's permission are different. In particular, fair dealing for the purposes of research or private study does not extend to research for commercial purposes.

The obtaining, recording, use and disclosure of personal data is governed by the Data protection Act 1998.

Material on the internet and copyright

Under UK law copyright material sent over the internet or stored in web servers will generally be protected in the same way as material in other media. .Anyone wishing to put copyright material on the internet, or distribute or download material that others have placed on the internet, should ensure that they have permission of the owners of the rights in the material unless copyright exceptions apply. Copyright will automatically protect any original literary, artistic or musical works placed on a web site. It is recommended that material is marked with the copyright symbol ©, your name, and date so it can be seen by anyone linking to any page of a site.

Copyright in software and multimedia

There are a number of key organisations representing rights holders in these areas:

Software

- The British Computer Society
- Business Software Alliance
- Educational Software Publishers Association
- Free Software Foundation Europe
- Intellect
- The European Leisure Software Publishers Association (ELSPA)
- The Federation Against Software Theft

Multimedia

British Interactive Multimedia Association Limited

Semi-conductor topographies

The layout design of a semi-conductor chip, or its topography, is protected in the UK under design right law. All countries that are members of the World Trade Organisation have an obligation to provide protection for semi-conductor topographies by some means.

Copyright exceptions to use of material on the internet

There is no specific copyright exception applying to copyright material on the internet but many of the general copyright exceptions might apply to material that has been published in this way. Some of the more relevant exceptions that might apply to use of material on the internet might be the fair dealing exceptions and also the educational exceptions.

In particular, the following might apply:

- 'Fair dealing' for the purposes of non-commercial research or private study might apply to a student or another person who downloads and uses material in their work, but it would be unlikely to cover giving the same material to a large number of people, such as all students in a class, and putting the material on the intranet. It does not apply at all to recordings of music or films.

- 'Fair dealing' for the purposes of criticism, review, or reporting events might apply where short passages of, or extracts from, copyright material are put on an intranet or even another internet website for these purposes, but it does not allow a photograph to be copied for news reporting

- The making of reprographic copies of published literary material by an educational establishment for the purposes of instruction might permit copies of materials that can be legally downloaded to be made for the whole class. But it does not allow for more than 1% of any copyright material to be copied and does not apply at all if the reprography is licensed. The Copyright Licensing Agency, The Newspaper Licensing Agency and Christian Copyright Licensing all offer licences, between them covering the copying of much published material.